T0148103

THE
NEW SPACE
GENESIS AND BACKGROUND

POLITICAL PHILOSOPHY, PHILOSOPHY, HUMANITIES.

FUNDAMENTALIST LIBERTY AND PLURALIST LIBERTY

THE
NEW SPACE
GENESIS AND BACKGROUND

BETWEEN VERTICAL LIBERTY AND HORIZONTAL RESPECT

BAHMAN BAZARGANI

iUniverse, Inc.
Bloomington

The New Space: Genesis and Background
Between Vertical Liberty and Horizontal Respect

iUniverse books may be ordered through booksellers or by contacting:

iUniverse
1663 Liberty Drive
Bloomington, IN 47403
www.iuniverse.com
1-800-Authors (1-800-288-4677)

ISBN: 978-1-4759-4779-3 (sc)
ISBN: 978-1-4759-4778-6 (hc)
ISBN: 978-1-4759-4777-9 (ebk)

Library of Congress Control Number: 2012917883

Printed in the United States of America

iUniverse rev. date: 09/25/2012

Contents

One

Today, it is a matter of fact when we say that, with the Islamic Revolution of Iran, fundamentalists overthrew the monarchy of Iran and so forth, we take it for granted that the fundamentalism defeated the nonfundamentalism. This is the story we repeatedly hear.

I was shocked by this observation that, during the turbulent period of 1970-1979 in Iran, there was an all-embracing trend to initiate to the fundamentalism and return to the origins—as if there were a consensus between nearly all the groups ranging from the monarchists to the Khomeinists about the return to our origins. This consensus prepared both of them to separate their ways from the West. This was easy for Khomeinists. They had nothing to do with the West and the Western way of the political/cultural life. As for monarchists, it was a radical shift from the pro-Western policy that they had adhered to after the father of the shah, who was regularly addressed in the official propaganda as the founder of the modern Iran.

Fundamentalism meant for the shah to return to the originality of the Iranian monarchic political model, with a "king of the kings" who, although not the God himself, explicitly was the real shadow of the God on the earth. What his majesty uttered was from the side of the God. The Great Cyrus, the founder of the Achaemenid dynasty about twenty-five hundred years ago, shaped this political system. At that period, the shah repeatedly hinted to the Western democratic civilization as a corrupt model that was on its way down. The shah, daresay, fully ignored his pro-Western consultants and dissolved or disintegrated most of the political institutions that were built during his father as well as his own rule and declared a one-party political system, as was in the Communist Bloc. At the same time, he was leading a strategy regarding the oil export policy in the OPEC that was not what his former allies and friends in the West were expecting.

I use the term "quasi-aesthetic focus/center of attraction" of a space/paradigm to distinguish this center that attracts all the people living in that space/paradigm. Hence, this constitutes the necessary precondition for a consensus out of their material interests, avowed aims, will, and consciousness from the other attractions, which attract a fraction of the people and hence could not constitute a base for the overall unanimity and consensus. This is somehow near to the sense of beauty, as it was in the time of Kant. That is why I prefer to use the term "quasi-aesthetic attraction."

In that period, fundamentalism had a quasi-aesthetic attraction in Iran so that many of the Iranian writers and philosophers had already initiated to the fundamentalism. *Gharb Zedegi (West-haunted-ness)*, a Samizdat book circulating between the intelligentsia as well as the Khomeinists, paradoxically was written by the prominent avant-garde writer J. Ale Ahmad, an ex-member of the communist party (Tudeh Party) and a veteran of the social democracy for Iran. His book was a daring expression of the vast anti-Western sentiments spreading all over in Iran. Ali Shariati's books also invited the young Muslims to initiate to the simplicity and originality as well as the socialistic tradition in some of the disciples of the prophet fourteen hundred years ago. At the same time, Dariush Shayegan, an Iranian philosopher, was emphasizing the Asian/Eastern moral values vis-à-vis the material values of the West. Ehsan Neraghi, another scholar with close relations with the royal court (Farah Pahlavi), was reiterating the same themes.

Two

This book is the development of the concepts introduced for the first time (2002) in the second chapter of *The Matrix of Beauty*.[1]

---

[1]   Bahman Bazargani, *Matris-e Zibaee (The Matrix of Beauty)* (Tehran: 2002).

In my life, I have experienced several lifestyles, as I have noted in the About the Author section. In each lifestyle, I saw so many unbelievable sides of man that we can name each package of these lifestyles as an independent space. In each of these spaces, there is a package of unquestionable beliefs that, at best, could be regarded as the myth/truth of that space that they may not be valid in the other spaces. In each space, a quasi-aesthetic focus of attraction attracts all. That is why I am so interested in the long-term social tendencies and biases that specify one paradigm/space from another.

I started with this assumption that, in each paradigm/space, a focus of attraction attracts all the people living in that paradigm/space independent of their interests, will, and consciousness. What is a beautiful or aesthetic case in one space could be ugly and obscene in another. We may remind the period that a quasi-aesthetic focus of attraction during the Third Reich haunted the whole nation in Germany. Love and hate in a terrorist/militarist are the Janusian faces of the same character. So what I mean as the quasi-aesthetic attraction can be applied to both life-full actions and to mortal deeds at the same time. It depends on where we are, from which space we are looking, and which focus of quasi-aesthetic attraction has attracted us.

So I was curious to interpret the cultural paradigms. The quasi-aesthetic focus of attraction worked to constitute a consensus at any paradigm, and this very fact imposed a huge impact over all the other aspects of their social life. Some parts of these impacts are briefly explored in the first chapter of this book in order to show how the quasi-aesthetic focus of attraction or metavalue overshadows all the other aspects of the social life during a paradigm.

In the first chapter of this book, I start with this assumption that the quasi-aesthetic focus of attraction of the polytheistic era was the brave hero. This quasi-aesthetic focus of attraction overshadows all the other parameters of that paradigm. What Homer was narrating in the *Iliad* was the act of adoring the heroes. Liberty, for example, in that paradigm meant the liberty of moving in three dimensions. During the monotheistic paradigm, the meaning of liberty was drastically changed and overshadowed by the quasi-aesthetic focus of attraction of that paradigm that is by the eternity/other world. I would like to show to the reader that it was the urge for the liberation of man's soul from the evil that the upward salvation arises as the meaning of liberty in the monotheistic paradigm. In the first chapter, I say that the defeat of the crusaders paved the way for the overall desperation in the middle age of the Europe. In *The Matrix of Beauty*, I repeatedly declare that "desperation is the clinical sign of the change of the matrix of beauty."

In the second chapter, I try to show that the era of reason was somehow an autocratic era that had a great impression upon the modern time while it was philosophically more tolerant the two centuries before. In the third chapter, I try to convince the reader that the arise of the nature for the first time in England as a new focus of the quasi-aesthetic attraction was quite a new factor in that time that paved the way for a real revolution in the science. In the fourth chapter, we have a new factor, the idea of the balance of the defying forces, a modern concept of a dynamic world vis-à-vis the old concept of the static world of Aristotle.

Chapter 5 is somehow out of the classic teachings of the political philosophy. Here J. J. Rousseau is portrayed as the founder of the fundamentalist school of the vertical liberty vis-à-vis the anti-authoritarian concepts of Locke. Here, liberty, according to me, is a new quasi-aesthetic focus of attraction, which as a metavalue and the "true" meaning of life, overshadows all the other social values.

In the sixth chapter, I concentrate on the crisis of the liberty. The crisis of liberty, according to me, is the symptom of the fact that, although there is a consensus on the liberty as the meaning of life, there is no consensus on the meaning of liberty. Here, the interpretations of communism and liberalism from the real meaning of liberty are juxtaposed. The aim of this juxtaposition is to show the Janusian character of the quasi-aesthetic focus of attraction. While it is a unifying center via all the social elements and groups into a deep consensus out of their material interests, will, and consciousness between themselves, at the same time, based on the metavalue of this consensus, they try to convince each other that their material interests and aims are legitimate. In order to do this, they start to manipulate the structure of the sentences and even the reasoning itself.

In the seventh chapter, I try to show that the political philosophy of the modern age is anyway inherited by Rousseau's ideas. That is why even the liberal philosophers such as Rawls and Rorty cannot trespass it's redlines. The book ends at a point that it seems that I intend to suggest that the horizontal respect is a new principle that will be the new quasi-aesthetic focus of attraction and a metavalue that would overshadow all the social values, even liberty itself. This is the beginning of the new space, pluralist mega space, or PMS.

ONE

VERTICAL LIBERTY
(UPWARD SALVATION)

Transition from the age of polytheism or, according to the Church, the age of paganism to the age of monotheism, coincides with a psychological revolution and discovery of self. It seems that man's revelation on monotheism was the consequence of this psychological revolution that paved the way for the conception of the vertical salvation, the mentality of the crave for the eternity, and finally the total change of the meaning of liberty.

In polytheism, everything is generated from a god/goddess that is its root and creator. When we fear, Phoebus does so. When we love, Eros has taken over us. Music and euphonious sounds are the work of Apollo and so forth.

What about me? What do I do here? It seems that there is no "I" or "self" that is involved in here. Self and I, in today's connotation, can be the products of monotheism. The "I" that fears, loves, plays, and composes, that "I" with these many positive/negative faculties, is inside me. This interior that is the source and reservoir of these many things and what we take as "self" can be the discovery/innovation of the monotheism. It looks like that, in polytheistic cultures, there is no interior/self either in gods or man. Gods look like monolithic and solid creatures. The god of love and the god of wrath act in such a way as if they are solid love or solid wrath. We may confer that, in the polytheistic era, the gods are the incarnation of eternal love or eternal wrath and so forth. And man is the god's playful doll. That is why polytheistic man is a playful man playing the god's game. And life is

1

nothing but fulfillment of one's destiny. But the wisest people, those who are Apollo's favorite, are play readers. They read the gods' plays and discern their intentions sooner than anyone else.

In polytheism, the moral dos and don'ts do not exist by today's meaning. Each god has his or her own redlines that you should be careful not to cross, lest you violate some taboos. Because in polytheism it is supposed that I am void of interior, therefore, contrary to monotheism, no question is ever asked about my good or bad intention. Therefore, regardless of my intention, the relevant punishment awaits me. Of course, in many cases, there is a way out that usually comes with redemption or sacrifice. But there is no tolerance.

Leniency and tolerance about the unwanted sins of the believers are the products of monotheism. They are totally performed with regard to the quality of interior. In monotheism, in most of the cases, it is a rule that, if I commit a sin unwillingly and without any previous intention, I can hope to be considered for leniency. Polytheism is the space of action while monotheism is essentially an inbound and intention-oriented space. Intention in the monotheism is very important. It is more important than the action, which comes after it. But interior is always full of different ideas and intentions. This abundance and diversity of ideas and intentions are inherent in the human mind. Man, when he discovered the abundance and diversity of ideas and intentions in the reservoir of his mind and when he was forced to attribute them to his self, which now was a new source of authority, found herself on a formidable precipice because, contrary to the limited and stricter kind of the pluralism of polytheism, monotheism is a monistic space that there is only one way to what they call liberation/salvation, but there are several ways to what they brand as fall and decline. They interpret the unity as the manifestation of the god while they interpret the multiplicity as the manifestation of evil.

By discovering the interior and concentrating on man's self, monotheism directed man to the source of a formidable potential power. But man had to pay a heavy price for it.

Charles Taylor says that liberty according to Hobbes is freedom of movement in three directions.[2] So the free man (not slave) of polytheism was almost free, even though he attributed his feelings, thoughts, hopes, and desires to the gods. Liberty was neither his problem nor his desire. He was not sensitive to the liberty, as we mean of it. And at the same time, he was practically almost free. Even though there were many taboos and dos and don'ts from the point of view of sexual relations, the essence of sexual relation as the manifestation of fertility of the herd and abundance of crops was recommended by the gods, which reached its pinnacle of ritualistic importance in the traditional festivities of orgy. Youthfulness and heroism were some of its special features, and heroic tales are the heritage of those periods. Youth and youthfulness was the mark fecundity, and in many places, when a son of an aged king reached puberty, he had to pass on the crown to him. Local rulers or second-rate kings did this as well. In Shahnameh, Saam-e Nariman, the father of Zaal, surrenders his crown/diadem at the end of the wedding ceremonies of his son and leaves Nimrooz. The tragedies of Siavash and Isfandiyar are the reminiscence of the beginning of the end of those ancient rituals and the recalcitrance of old kings from the tradition of devolving the power to a young son. Women, by far, had much more freedom of action in social associations and played a unique role in many places, especially when they welcomed the strangers. After twenty years, Ulysses returns to Ithaca. Penelope, according to the local rites of hospitality, when washing him, sees a sign in his body and recognizes him. In Shahnameh, Tahmineh, and Manizheh easily intercourse with Rostam and Bijan, respectively, and no one calls Sohrab, son of Rostam and Tahmineh, an illegal son of Rostam. Heroes and warriors boast in banquets and battles. Literature of ancient times is full of poems that heroes compose when introducing and stunting themselves.

---

[2] Charles Taylor, "What's Wrong with Negative Liberty?" (1979), in *Philosophical Papers* (volume 2) (Cambridge University Press, 1999).

In Greece, in the age of Pericles, liberty was not related to the public sphere:

> In the words that Thucydides puts in his mouth, Pericles says something like this: "in public we conduct the affairs of the city; as for the private, as for the affairs of the individual, we leave those be handled as each person thinks fit."[3]

Hayek says,

> The first people who had clearly formulated the ideal of individual liberty were the ancient Greeks and particularly the Athenians . . . Their conception of freedom was of freedom under the law, or of a state of affairs in which, as the popular phrase ran, law was king. It found expression, during the early classical periods, in the ideal of *isonomia* or equality before the law which, without using the old name, is still clearly described by Aristotle.[4]

The gregarious and objective-minded man of polytheism became the introvert and subjective man of monotheism. Which center of attraction hypnotized and pulled him as such that he left all of those enthusiasms of polytheism and became such fixated on the attractions of the monotheism that all those extroversions and objectivity was not seen other than a useless wandering and wasting of time in wrong paths ending in darkness?

This is the attraction of eternity. In this new space, man is so mesmerized with the attraction of immortality and reaches to such a degree of enchantment about eternity that whatever is mortal, malleable, and unstable, from man's life to the beauty of flowers and

---

3   Jacque Ranciere, *On the Shores of Politics*, trans. Liz Heron (2007), 40.
4   F.A. Hayek, *New Studies in the Philosophy, Politics, Economics and the History of Ideas* (Routledge & Kegan Paul, 1978), 122.

seasons, no longer has any value for him. He believes that immortality does not belong to this world but in the other world in which there is no place for senescence, wilt, decay, and death. All the ways other than immortality and eternity end in abyss. The polytheistic world was one world. The gods were living in the same world with man. The eternal world is a different world. In Chinese and Indian cultures, the other world and that concept of god that exists in the Semitic cultures where that other world has no meaning without the existence of god does not have much a role. But these cultures are also obsessed with eternity.

An exit from the age of polytheism and entry into the age of monotheism, as I interpret it, was the consequence of a quasi-aesthetic revolution that subjectivity superseded the objectivity. It would be more precise to say that a new paradigm defined everything anew and with totally different criterion. And almost for the first time, man concentrates all his attention on the reservoir of subjectivity and its amazing byproducts. In the new paradigm, the bodily world of the polytheism was divided into two worlds: the material world and the ethereal world. Man ended up having two of his selves: one subjective and dependent on soul and susceptible to ascend and salvation and the other objective and dependent body and with a constant inclination to fall and decay respectively. In his *Meditations*, St. Augustine concludes he has two kinds of self: one incarnation of light, perfection, and transcendence and the other immanent and the marketplace of passions.

In the stratification of Middle Ages, the above and sky is sublime. The highest part of sky, the supreme empyrean, is the place of excellence and eternity. This stratification is not fundamentally different from the Aristotelian stratification in which heavy bodies drop downward and light bodies ascend upward. According to the Semitic myths, man was created by the council of God and from the soil of the earth by the hand of God blowing His breath into the lips of man. It did not take long for this contradictory creature to collapse from its heavenly place down to the earth. By Aristotelian interpretation, this descent of the body of man down to the earth comes from the internal inclination of the body to descend to the earth. By this interpretation, the motive of the original sin and Eve's temptation is the earthly pull that the body of man is built from. But after the descent, a reverse trend begins. Now the soul of man is in the throes of returning to its origin in the celestial world.

This stratification is not simply a Semitic myth or mixture of Egyptian, Semitic, or Greek myths. Rather, it is a lasting belief that has stamped its indelible mark not only in a formal and obvious manner throughout the Middle Ages but also by an implicit and half-hidden manner over the whole Age of Reason. It might be difficult to understand the Christian culture of the Middle Ages and moral etiquettes of the Age of Reason without this categorization. By the expansion of Christianity in Europe, this stratification was tied to Ptolemy's council and was weaved with the philosophies of Plato, Aristotle, and Plotinus. Although it has a positive value in the modern age, we may pay attention to the negative value of the word "matter": "Matter is therefore both cause of weakness in the soul and cause of sin. It is therefore itself antecedently evil and primary evil."[5]

But faith in God can mostly be based on love or mostly on reason. Usually depending upon the emphasis made on this or that, it is the notion of the existence of different schools. St. Augustine emphasizes faith-based love; St. Thomas Aquinas emphasizes faith-based reason.

The word "liberty" in the Middle Ages had a totally different meaning from today's connotation, freedom from the bodily desires and the tight fence of imperious self. The Middle Ages place the same value for obedience to God and liberty: "My soul was liberated from the yoke[6] . . . Your soul can not be liberated but with knowledge and obedience."[7]

Obedience to God used to exalt man, and God's true believer always craved to liberate his self from caprice, impulse, and bodily desires. Therefore, in the etymology of the Middle Ages, God's servant and liberated man had the same connotation. A disciple used to try to

---

[5]   Lloyd P. Gerson, ed., "Plotinus," cf. the *Cambridge Companion to Plotinus* (Cambridge University Press, 1996), 185.

[6]   Nasir Khusraw, *Encyclopedia of Dehkhoda.*

[7]   Ibid.

liberate his self from the burden of bodily desires. The believer who would reach this level of freedom deserved to be God's servant. Such a servant who was liberated was full of dos, don'ts, duty, and mission. Centuries later, the Age of Reason confiscated the word "liberty" for its own good, placed it on a path different from its Middle Ages, and gave it a different meaning, but it saved that pyramidal structure of value intertwined with it and mounted the dos, don'ts, missions, and duties comparable to the Age of Reason on it. Today, that pyramidal structure is disintegrated. Not only has the meaning of the word "liberty" somehow become the opposite of its Middle Ages meaning, it has even become strange to its meaning in the Age of Reason. A substantial part of that lifestyle that was synonymous with satanic lifestyle in the Middle Ages now has come forth and become the standard and criterion of humanity.

Despair and Bewilderment Is the Sign of the Structural Change in the Matrix of Beauty[8]

At the end of the Crusades, a huge despair and bewilderment spread in Christian Europe that ultimately led to a fundamental change in the attitude toward God and the other world on one hand and to man and nature on the other. At the end of the Middle Ages, the former ideals and maxims no longer were attractive, a bodily man appeared instead of the heaven-oriented man, and the tendency for an spiritual ascend to above and heaven transformed into a tendency to believe in surface circumnavigation. Living in convent, contentment, piety, and retraction from sins were no longer attractive and fascinating.

During the Renaissance, the old moralities were still officially credible, but they were not heeded. Even the lords of the Church were practically stranger to religious morals, such that we do not see much of a difference between the behaviors of popes and that of princes in those periods. The political conducts of popes were closer

---

[8]   Bahman Bazargani, (*The Matrix of Beauty*), 221.

to Machiavelli's lessons than to the commandments of the Holy Book. Officially, the assumption was that everyone should adhere to the religious morals. They didn't. The old values and morals were not negated. They simply lacked attraction. Thus, the ecclesiastical beliefs, without being defeated by the rival beliefs, evidently became secure and untouched but forlorn and hollow. Now, man, certainly the willful elite man, radiates:

> Pico della Mirandella in his speech on the dignity of man, which may justly be called one of the noblest bequests of that great age, God he tells us, made man at the close of creation, to know the laws of the universe, to love its beauty, to admire its greatness[9] ... God does not want to do everything, so as not to take free will from us and that part of the glory that falls to us.[10]

Now the Middle Ages meaning of liberty had lost its attraction. Liberty was distanced from the old topics of ascend/descent, and a new trend toward the expansion in surface and believing in the surface were giving a totally different meaning to liberty, free will.

The Middle Ages had a negative attitude toward the freedom of will. They believed that such a will was not credible because it could lead man against providence. It seems that, from Dante's time, the ground for the attractiveness of will would be gradually accommodated:

> What stirs you if the senses show you nothing?
> Light stirs you, formed in Heaven, by itself,
> Or by His will Who sends it down to us:[11]

---

[9] Jacob Burckhardt, *Civilization of the Renaissance in Italy*, 185.
[10] Niccolo Machiavelli, *The Prince*, second edition, trans. Harvey C. Mansfield (Chicago: University of Chicago Press, 1998), 103.
[11] Dante Alighieri, *Divine Comedy, Purgatury*, canto 17.

The attractions of the Middle Ages that the saints were at its apex left the public sphere and entered the private spaces. When piety, abstinence, and monasticism left the stage, free will became attractive. Of course, only the elite could benefit from that. The elite man of the Renaissance, whose attention and concentration was in riding the surface, as we may call him a "surface rider," enthusiastically grasped the pleasure, power, and wealth. Discovering far, distant lands that were the ready baits for looting as the source of derelict gold, jewelry, and spice gave a new energy to the adventurous surface riders. They did not use the words "discovery" and "discoverer" by chance. Some attractions in these words referred to the discoverer's free will.

Humanists turned their eyes from the sky and heaven down to earth and man. Now they could enjoy the taste of pleasure. But what they meant of man was not the general public, and the idea of equality of men was not attractive at all. They looked with a contemptuous eye toward the mass of people. For the humanists, man's free will meant the will of the elite, and at its head was the prince, who, according to Machiavelli, could and should look to God, morality, and people with a utilitarian eye and is authorized to employ everything for solidifying foundations of His power.

The Crisis of Faith

The sixteenth century had incorporated inharmonious doctrines who were engaged in a silent battle over the leadership of the European culture. Every doctrine had his own interpretation of the past as well his own anticipation of the future. The principles Machiavelli put forth were essential for safeguarding the political power. When we enter the power game, Machiavelli advises us that neither ethics, religion, nor age-old traditions of the aristocracy marked the rules of the political games. This very reason for safeguarding the political power dictated its own rules. This was a doctrine among many, which existed parallel to each other, next to each other, and crossing each other in the semipluralism of the sixteenth century, and in that practical pluralist space, each was relatively attractive.

Isaiah Berlin, on the importance of Machiavelli, says,

> This unifying monistic pattern is at the very heart of traditional rationalism, religious and atheistic, metaphysical and scientific, transcendental and naturalistic, that has been characteristic of Western civilization. It is this rock, upon which Western beliefs and lives had been founded, that Machiavelli seems, in effect, to have split open. So great a reversal cannot, of course, be due to the acts of a single individual[12] . . . Many beside him, medieval nominalists and secularists, Renaissance humanists, doubtless supplied their share of the Dynamite . . . it was Machiavelli who lit the fatal fuse.[13]

But this is Berlin's judgment in the twentieth century. If Berlin were a contemporary of Descartes, he would not have attributed such an epoch making role to Machiavelli. "This rock, upon which Western beliefs and lives had been founded," showed many cracks in the sixteenth century was restored and hardened in the seventeenth century, and Machiavelli was forgotten as well. Machiavellism was the consequence of skepticism and relativism, even at a time when church and moral values of the aristocracy had lost their attractions to a large extent. When we come to the Age of Reason, we should respect what those people meant from the words like "reason" and "rational." They did not take Machiavelli's teachings as rational. No wonder that, after the establishment of the Age of Reason, Machiavelli was forgotten, and until two centuries later, nothing was left of Machiavellism other than a "disgraceful" mark.

The contemporary political philosophy exaggerates when it evaluates the realm of Machiavelli's effects over the later centuries. This exaggeration is based on the high importance, which, in the

---

[12]   John Gray, *Berlin* (Fontana Press, 1995), 48.
[13]   Ibid., page 48.

contemporary academic tradition, is attributed to the virtue of the precedence of composition of a theory without paying any attention to this fact that the precedence of composition of a theory is not enough for the priority of its impact in that period or later eras. In the history of thought, we find very few cases where a theory impacts other periods by having precedence over that era. Rather, new theories usually arrive as a package and along with prologues and epilogues that often are not neutral. So long as they are not attractive, they do not get absorbed. Machiavelli and Machiavellism, at least in the Age of Reason, were abandoned, and it is not known whether those who were practically Machiavellist had even read Machiavelli. Every generation has many practical Machiavellists without Machiavelli.

However, we must respect the notions of the past thinkers. When they themselves justify their theories without any reference to Machiavelli and we do not find enough credible evidence on the impact of the extent of Machiavelli's theories on later periods, we should not exaggerate it simply because of the similarity of their irreligious approach and secular points of view and by the emphasis in which Machiavelli has precedence over them. Berlin too emphasizes that the very trend of political and moral philosophers in the West have not been much impacted by Machiavelli: "His works were pronounced immoral and condemned by the church, and not taken altogether seriously by the moralists and political thinkers who represent the central current of western thought in these fields."[14]

But we must confess that we find the best model of the theory of elitist individualism, which the humanist movement in Machiavelli generates. The important point in here is the reconstruction of the main aspects of that sphere. At that time, the grandeur and its generated pride had an exceptional attraction. Today, words like "grandeur" and "pride" are bankrupt. But the people of that period were craving grandeur and splendor. Individualism at that time could not thrive unless it was associated with an aspect of eternity and

---

[14]   Isaiah Berlin, *The Crooked Timber of Humanity*, ed. Henry Hardy (London: Pimlico, 2003), 31.

grandeur. Such a man in some respect was the successor to God, and this was exactly the thing that would ultimately limit the development of individualism and would not allow to develop for a similar situation like that of today for the expansion of individualism.

Hobbes finds crave for splendor to come from man's intrinsic motivating forces, a force that stands against the necessities of social life.[15] At that time, "the individual is unconstrained by any social bonds. His own ends—not only those of power, but also those of glory and reputation—are for him the only criteria of action."[16] Grandeur, splendor, pomp, and their consequence, that is, the pride, were the goals that freedom of will had to erect.

> With or without such sophisticated justification, striving for honor and glory was exalted by the medieval chivalric ethos even though it stood at odds with the central teachings, not only of St. Augustine, but of a long line of religious writers, from St. Thomas Aquinas to Dante, who attacked glory-seeking as both vain and sinful. Then, during the Renaissance, the striving for honor achieved the status of a dominant ideology as the influence of church receded and the advocates of the aristocratic ideal were able to draw on the plentiful Greek and Roman texts celebrating the pursuit of glory. This powerful intellectual current carried over into the seventeenth century: perhaps the purest conception of glory-seeking as the only justification of life is to be found in the tragedies of Corneille.[17]

---

[15] K.A. Appiah, "Identity, Authenticity, Survival: Multicultural Societies and Social Reproduction," in *Multiculturalism*, ed. Amy Gutmann (Princeton University Press, 1994), 160.

[16] Alasdair MacIntyre, *A Short History of Ethics* (Routledge, 1998), 124.

[17] Albert O. Hirschman, *The Passions and the Interests—Political Arguments for Capitalism before Its Triumph* (Princeton University Press, 1977), 10-11.

Charles Taylor writes, "[T]he collapse of social hierarchies, which used to be the basis for honor . . . As against this notion of honor, we have the modern notion of dignity, now used in a universalist and egalitarian sense."[18]

Machiavelli's prince was Nietzsche's superman with his political "gay science." While Machiavelli praises the grandeur of ancient Rome, he sees the morale ideals of the ancient world as impractical and emphasizes on the deep rift that exists between reality and ideals: "One will find something appears to be virtue, which if pursued would be one's ruin, and something else appears to be vice, which if pursued results in one's security and well-being."[19]

Although humanism deeply influenced Machiavelli, his doctrines can be considered as a farewell to moral ideals of humanism. What Machiavelli asserted was the audacious formulation of the prevailing behavior of the time:

> The nature of peoples is variable[20] . . . And men have less hesitation to offend one who makes himself loved than one who makes himself feared; for love is held by a chain of obligation, which, because men are wicked, is broken at every opportunity for their own utility, but fear is held by a dread of punishment that never forsakes you.[21]

Machiavelli's ideas, which theoretically and practically were limited to the prince and his rule, could not find a suitable ground of acceptance in the seventeenth century because there was no place among the developing values with new rationalism for the candidness

---

[18] Charles Taylor, "The Politics of Recognition" (1992), in *Multiculturalism—Examining the Politics of Recognition* (Princeton, 1994), 27. In the same place in the footnote, Charles Taylor refers to Peter Berger's article, "On the Obsolescence of the Concept of Honour." Michael Sandel also cites Berger's article in *Liberalism and Its Critics*.

[19] Machiavelli, *The Prince*, 62.

[20] Ibid., 24.

[21] Ibid., 66.

of Machiavelli's word. Machiavellism remained in the realm of action but was suppressed in the realm of theory. A cloak of virtue was draped around the sculpture of power. Machiavelli himself should have predicated this because Machiavellism is a two-edged sword that could also cut the hands of its owner. Thus, Machiavelli was damned until the nineteenth century and only after Hegel and even a suitable ground for a different impression from Machiavelli was slowly accommodated. But until recently was the label of Machiavellism continued to be used as a euphemism for political curse.

Not only was the political and moral crisis of that period shown in Machiavelli's prince, the revolt of the rural mob that Luther unwillingly inspired was another side of it. Luther hoped his ideas would be limited by the framework he outlined. But the vacuum created by the elimination of the Vatican in the realm of society inevitably expanded the extent of the impact of the rebellious forces and theories that were no more desirable for Luther.

In art and especially in painting and architecture, clear vein of crises were also developing. Rebellious artists wanted to change the tradition of the time. They were "infatuated" by the centrifugal revelations. Although Michelangelo did not go far in deracinating the orthodoxy, he was the originator of this new path:

> Michelangelo in particular had occasionally shown a bold disregard for all conventions-nowhere more than in architecture, where he sometimes abandoned the sacrosanct rules of classical tradition to follow his own moods and whims. It was he himself who accustomed the public to admire the artist's "caprices" and "inventions" and who set the example of a genius not satisfied with the matchless perfection of his own early masterpieces, but constantly and restlessly searching for new methods and modes of expression.[22]

---

[22]   E.H. Gombrich, *The Story of Art* (Phaidon Press Limited, 1995), 278.

We find the same spirit in the paintings of ... Parmigianino (1503-40) . . . The picture is called the "Madonna with the long neck" because the painter, in his eagerness to make the Holy Virgin look graceful and elegant, has given her a neck like that of a swan. He has stretched and lengthened the proportions of the human body in a strangely capricious way. The hand of the Virgin with its long delicate fingers, the long leg of the angel in the foreground, the lean, haggard prophet with a scroll of parchment, we see them all as through a distorting mirror. And yet there can be no doubt that the artist achieved this effect through neither ignorance nor indifference. He has taken care to show us that he liked these unnaturally elongated forms, for, to make doubly sure of his effect, he placed an oddly shaped high column of equally unusual proportions in the background of the painting.[23]

Rawls says that, at that period, "It [Reformation] fragmented the religious unity of the Middle Ages and led to religious pluralism, with all its consequences for later centuries. This in turn fostered pluralism of other kinds, which were a permanent feature of culture by the end of the eighteenth century."[24]

We know the suppression of centrifugal and anti-monistic tastes began by the bulldozer of the Age of Reason and these disturbing therapies and iconoclastic innovations were quenched in their embryo. Here we may remind Montaigne (1533-1592), the most striking of skepticism and relativism of this period. Skepticism and relativism thrived by humanism and became a reality among the humanists whom could not be ignored. Those two rebellious elements had a tumultuous impact in that era because, not only were they the theoretical manifestation of melee and disbelief of that time,

---

[23]   Ibid., 280-281.

[24]   John Rawls, *Political Liberalism* (1993), (New York: Colombia University Press, 1996), xxiv.

they were also the symbol of crisis among the clerics and scholars. It was as if Greek sophists were reborn after almost two thousand years.

> Seeking the security of absolute certainty for his philosophy was not simply an attractive luxury for Descartes. The attacks on the Aristotelianism of the schools, which had become so frequent by the early seventeenth century, had produced a fearsome armory of argumentative weapons. The most lethal, particularly in France, where they had proven especially popular, were the weapons of philosophical skepticism. . . . that were adopted so eagerly in the second half of the sixteenth century and beginning of the seventeenth . . . known as Pyrrhonism (named after the supposed founder of this philosophical position, Pyrrhon of Elis) . . . Pyrrhonian skepticism was one of the weapons that had been successfully used to weaken the hold of Aristotelian philosophy . . . Scepticism of this sort was therefore a line of attack against which Descartes wanted his own philosophy to be secure.[25]

Descartes assumed the responsibility to end skepticism and relativism as a sensitive and solemn duty. He used a special technique. He armed himself with the weapon of the adversary and broke and neutralized it, a technique that Kant also used against Hume in the next two centuries.

We often begin with this prejudice as if the main challenge of the Age of Reason were confrontation against the suppression of the church and scholasticism. In the seventeenth century, scholasticism was void of vigor and attraction. Within the power structure of the time was exercising quite a period of crisis of that time.

---

[25] Peter Dear, *Revolutionizing the Sciences: European Knowledge and Its Ambitions, 1500-1700* (Princeton University Press, 2001), 82-83.

A radically different situation obtained during the 17th century. Not only were the universities of Europe not the foci of scientific activity, not only did natural science have to develop its own centers of activity independent of the universities, but the universities were the principal centers of opposition to the new conception of nature which modern science constructed.[26]

Descartes did not have a major problem with scholasticism. Rather, his serious problem was the confrontation he had with the growing skepticism and relativism. Even scholasticism as well, after two centuries of difficult challenge against the skepticism and relativism, was exhausted, and scholastics themselves too were not immune from these viruses. The silent and, more or less, half-hidden struggle between these two rebellious elements and the thriving rationalism was much more fundamental than the clamorous and theatrical battle between rationalism and scholasticism plus the Church. Even though scholasticism and church still had power, they were not attractive. It is always between the attractive ideas and institutions that a silent but fundamental battle breaks out, and the winner of this silent battle grabs the power structure of the future as a reward. But when the victor of the battle starts writing the history, he recalls that side of the battle that is beneficial to him. In the history of sciences and philosophy written after Descartes, there was a lot of emphasis on the trial of Galileo by the Church. It was as if there were no skeptics and relativists.

Reason's Field of Attraction

From the very first genesis of the monotheistic religions, faith and reason, as the two complementing factors like two limbs or legs

---

[26] Keith Thomas, *Religion & Decline of Magic* (1971) (New York: Charles Scribner's Son), 105.

that were necessary and required, had a relentless rivalry over the hegemony and leadership.

Saint Augustine, despite being a rationalist, was well aware that giving the priority to reason over faith at the time he lived places the lessons of Greek philosophy in a better situation with respect to the ecclesiastical tenets, especially in the disputable cases like the creation or age of universe. This was meant to sow the seeds of doubt among believers. But that old rivalry benefited the reason at the end of the Crusades. The emphasis on reason had begun at the end of the Middle Ages, and Saint Thomas Aquinas theorized that trend. I may dare to say that the efforts of Aquinas and his followers in reconciling faith and reason was an indication that, with the dusk of religious faith, reason was ascending.

Rawls, in his introduction to *Political Liberalism*, lists five characteristics for the Middle Ages' Christianity (characteristics that civil religion does not have):

> It tended towards an authoritarian religion: its authority—the Church itself headed by the papacy—was institutional, central, and nearly absolute, although the supreme authority of the pope was sometimes challenged, as in the conciliar period of the fourteenth and fifteenth centuries. It was a religion of salvation, a way to eternal life, and salvation required true belief as the Church taught it. Hence, it was a doctrinal religion with a creed that was to be believed. It was a religion of priests with the sole authority to dispense means of grace, means normally essential to salvation. Finally, it was an expansionist religion of conversion that recognized no territorial limits to its authority short of the world as a whole.[27]

---

[27] Rawls, *Political Liberalism*, xxv.

When Luther introduced the Christian faith as the connecting link between a devout individual with God and deprived the Church and pope from the privilege of monopoly with God, maybe without realizing its fargoing consequences, he catapulted the religious faith into the private spaces and paved the way for the reason to ascend as the prince of public sphere. This accident, which took place surreptitiously in the sixteenth century a few decades later, helped reason to locate itself as the protagonist of a new stage during the seventeenth and eighteenth centuries.

In the Middle Ages, from the orthodox ecclesiastical point of view, economic activity was regarded as the necessary evil. But in the sixteenth century, a devout Christian became a man whose utmost duty was maximal effort for economic activity. This paved the way for emergence of the school of the utilitarianism.

The blow with which Luther, by freeing the Christian man from the yoke of pope and the pronouncement of equality for Christians in front of God struck to the prejudicial Middle Ages church hierarchy, had a tremendous impact. Throughout centuries, the Church had inculcated this belief in the minds that nobility and priests are God's chosen providence and natural order that must direct and supervise the shepherd like *hoi polloi* demos in worldly and heavenly matters, respectively. Ecclesiastically speaking, some people naturally have higher prestige over others. That is, people did not have an equal status in front of God. Rebellious teachings of Luther, despite all their contradictions, shattered this long-lasting belief.

MacIntyre believes "Machiavelli and Luther mark in their different ways the break with the hierarchical, synthesizing society of the Middle Ages, and the distinctive moves into the modern world. In both writers there appears a figure who is absent from moral theories in periods when Plato and Aristotle dominate it, the figure of individual."[28] MacIntyre names Machiavelli the Luther of the secular sphere.[29]

---

[28]   MacIntyre, *A Short History of Ethics*, 117.
[29]   Ibid., 122.

Now Christians were freed from the Vatican's dependence and became equal before God. With this important step, liberty, in its limited connotation, and equality, again by its limited connotation of equality between devout Christians, became active and affective ideas. Next to the vertical respect, which was the only form of respect by that time, also provided the grounds for the emergence of the horizontal respect, that is, mutual respect between equal people.

Two

Dictatorship and Cartesian Reason

Wherever universal truth has been established,
there is no room for negotiation.[30]

We won't be able to reach to the roots of authoritarian attitude of modernity unless we recognize the deep impact that the authoritarian attitude of the beginning of the modern age has had on our impression, which we are still the beneficiary of.

The reason and rationality that became the dominant discourse of the eighteenth century evidently was propounding a new criteria and a new authority against the authority of church, a new authority that at first relied on the authoritarian kings who had secular tendencies and could balance the church's authority. By moving from the seventeenth to the eighteenth century, the Church was weakened and no longer a serious threat. That discourse took another step forward and placed the natural laws that were assumed as universal and eternal, first implicitly and then explicitly, against the arbitrary laws of the rulers and kings. Up to this time, the sovereignty was traditionally perceived as a divine decree that was hierarchically ordained from God to king and from king to the people. But now it appears as a social contract.

---

[30] Michael Walzer, "Philosophy and Democracy," in *Debates in Contemporary Political Philosophy: An Anthology,* ed. M. Matravers and J. Pike (Routledge, 2003), 375.

Two centuries from the middle of the fifteenth century (the fall of Constantinople) until the middle of the seventeenth century (end of the Thirty Years' War of religions) is a unique epoch in some ways. Rival theories and values were standing face to face. Those two centuries had a totally different sphere in contrast to the Middle Ages. Contrary to those two centuries, during the Age of Reason, that is, from the middle of the seventeenth century until the emergence of the Romantic Movement, belief in the omnipotence of reason received widespread acceptance. But at the end of this period, reason was interweaved with the power structure of the time to such an extent that, from the end of the nineteenth century, reason became the most fundamental factor of the economic, social, and political power structure.

It might not be far off if we say that, by the Age of Reason, even the free will of man needed the help of reason: "So that we easily extend it [will] beyond that which we apprehend clearly. And when we do this there is no wonder if it happens that we are deceived."[31]

Therefore, to prevent unlimited ambitions of the will, reason must bring the desires under its control:

> Descartes' essay on the passions of the soul and Spinoza's presentation of his doctrine of the affects in the third book of his *Ethics* are not simply occasional writings; they form integral parts of their systems . . . The clear and distinct idea, not the inarticulate affect, is characteristic of the real nature of the soul. Desires and appetites, the passions of sense, belong only indirectly to the soul; they are not its original properties and tendencies, but rather disturbances which the soul suffers as a result of its union with the body . . . Only that action has ethical value which overcomes these disturbances, which illustrate the

---

[31] Rene Descartes, "Principles of Philosophy," in *The Philosophical Works of Descartes* (volume 1), trans. Elizabeth S. Haldane, C.H., LL.D., G.R.T. Ross, M.A., and D. Phil.

triumph of the active over the passive part of the souls, of reason over the passions.[32]

Descartes's reason is a masculine one. "The bourgeois world instituted a moral attitude of labor between reason and sentiment, identifying masculinity with reason and femininity with sentiment, desire, and the needs of the body."[33]

Cartesian reason, the only effective and efficient instrument against the pluralist beliefs, was faced with the warm reception of the kings, and the Church and scholasticism, even though there were still mild critics, essentially tolerated it:

> Seventhly, you say not one word [in meditations] about the immortality of the human soul, which nevertheless you should above all things have proved and demonstrated as against those men—themselves unworthy of immortality—who completely deny it and perchance have an enmity against it.[34]

Peter Dear has something about this subject. Descartes's:

> [M]ajor concern, and the one that had persuaded him to suppress *Le Monde* in 1633, was the unorthodoxy (as defined by Galileo's trial) of holding that the earth is in motion. Descartes published the *Principles*, with its more elaborate version of the same world—picture as that of *Le Monde*, only once he had thought of a way to deny the

---

[32] Ernest Cassirer, *The Philosophy of Enlightenment*, trans. Fritz C.A. Koelln and James P. Pettegrove (Boston: Beacon Press, 1961), 105.

[33] Marion Young, "Polity and Group Difference: A Critic of the Ideal of Universal Citizenship," in *Contemporary Political Philosophy—An Anthology*, ed. R.E. Goodin and P. Pettit (Blackwell, 2002), 258.

[34] Father Mersenne, "Objections 2," in *The Philosophical Works of Descartes* (volume 2), trans. Elizabeth S. Haldane, C.H., LL.D. and G.R.T. Ross, M.A., and D. Phil.

movement of the earth without compromising any of his cosmology. The trick . . . was involved emphasizing the relativity of motion.[35,36]

Thus, Descartes acted very cautiously in relation with the Church on one hand and did the best service to the Church by suppressing skepticism and relativism on the other. Like Montaigne, Descartes also doubts, but his intention is different. Montaigne's doubt is an ontological doubt, precisely the same thing that Descartes wants to overthrow:

> Not that indeed I imitated the skeptics, who only doubt for the sake of doubting, and pretend to be always uncertain; for, on the contrary, my design was only to provide myself with good ground for assurance, and to reject the quicksand and mud in order to find the rock or clay.[37]

Descartes's skepticism had a predictable outcome. Descartes tries to categorize the subject he was interested in into clear and distinct units. It is not clear that, if Descartes would come to life, what kind of reaction he would have exhibited to John Rawls's veil of ignorance.

It is not inappropriate in here to read Voltaire's verdict about the unexpected consequences of Descartes's philosophy:

> When one is persuaded, with Descartes, that it is impossible for the universe to be finite, that the quantity

---

[35]   Peter Dear, *Revolutionizing the Sciences*, 96.

[36]   Ibid. [motion] "Is the difference of one piece of matter, or one body, from the vicinity of the other bodies which are in immediate contact with it. And which are regarded as being at rest to the vicinity of the other bodies."

[37]   Rene Descartes, "Discourse on the Method," in *The Philosophical Works of Descartes* (volume 1), trans. Elizabeth S. Haldane, C.H., LL.D., G.R.T. Ross, M.A., and D. Phil, 99.

of motion in the universe is ever equal and the same; when we presume to say, give me matter and motion and I will form a world; then, it must be confessed that these positions seem, by consequences too just, to exclude that of a Being sole infinite, sole author of motion, and sole author of the organization of substances.[38]

The Identity Crisis

The impact of the development of humanism was farfetched such that, in the sixteenth century, the identity crisis was a general dilemma because, contrary to the Middle Ages, man's identity no longer was dependent on the Church and God. There was uncertainty and confusion about the criterion, which, in practice, became the steamroller of an unwanted pluralism. The problem was that pluralism was not attractive at that time. On the contrary, its great rivals, eternity and monism, were attractive. That is why we find nothing left from that pluralism in the next century.

Germination of the individualism is often attributed to the Renaissance and the beginning of the modern world. But that individualism with the one that we understand from individualism today was very different. The portrait that was made from individual at that time was not the same individual who is familiar to us with all her limitedness, finitude, and unique character, one who chooses her personal moral, values, and dos and don'ts of her own private space. And by her death, everything would end. Of these factors that are now the main factors of individualism, none of them existed at that time. Rather, individual and individualism was under attention to such a degree that they would have a common denominator with reason, eternity, perfection, splendor, and pride. The individual in Descartes's/Kant's eye is not a unique and distinct individual from

---

[38] Voltaire, "Newtonian Nature," in *Great Trends in the History of Western Thought (Part Two)*, ed. Franklin Loofan Bomer, 405-406.

another individual. Rather, it is a typical and ideal one by virtue of his reason. At that time, they emphasized on reason as a distinguished specificity of his pride over the rest of the world, especially over the animals. This was not to denigrate animals because that was a fait accompli. The main aim was rather to create a new and different criterion from that of aristocracy for the social stratification and to segregate humans.

Descartes can be regarded as the Machiavelli of the Age of Reason. It is enough to look at reason in place of the prince. He almost confiscates everything from all the numerous resources for the interests of domination and sovereignty of reason. Cartesian reason introduced a new definition for the omnipotent and willful man of the Renaissance, which went beyond the limits of the humanist movement and opened a new age in which there was no place for the relativism and skepticism of the sixteenth century. Descartes erected his ontology on the originality of "cogito" amalgamated with the willful man of the sixteenth century who craved splendor and pride. With "cogito," Descartes placed him against the practical pluralist man of the previous century. The significance of Descartes's doctrine was based on his ontology, and with this new identity, the grounds for man's independence from the grip of religion and church were accommodated.

Assimilation of man's identity with his thought was the terminating point of the overall uncertainty and confusion of the time. Descartes did something that the Renaissance was unable to do despite its enormous extensiveness. The dilemma of man's identity now was solved. By grafting man's identity with his thought, the Archimedean relying stand was obtained. This was a unifying stand for all.

But the problem was that the sublime values were also in crisis. The identity crisis and the widespread crisis of values, in most cases, are simultaneous. When the new identity appears and it gathers consensus, the identity crisis also resolves, and at the same time, the widespread crisis of values declines. Normally, the emergence of the new identity and the generation of the new system of values or the new paradigm are inseparable. That is why that, after the emergence of the new identity, a consensus is quickly reached, and those who did not agree in its early stages stop the disagreements and reach a consensus. Those who remain adverse are soon abandoned and, unlike the past, are not tolerated.

Today, reason no more has the same qualities of the time of Descartes, and we have gotten used to realize that morals are independent from reason. In continental Europe, the separation of reason from morals started after the French Revolution and the rise of the Romantic Movement. But at the time of Descartes, reason had already monopolized man's system of strong values to the extent that the credibility of church's tenets had to be verified by it. We may say that at that time, "Serious reflection is *ipso facto* moral effort and involves a heightened sense of value and an attitude of perfection."[39] It means that, at that time, "Contemplation turns in to admiration, adoration, and joy."[40]

Although thought, according to Descartes, was a godly essence, but even for approaching God, one must initiate from thought. This was a new base that the modern world was founded on it, and by relying on this base, Descartes suppressed the pluralism, relativism, and skepticism. But this was only half of the truth.

Supreme Power as Originator

By starting from skepticism and reaching to the certainty that "it is me who thinks," Descartes answered the most important and urgent question of the time. Who am I as a man? This response swept the continent like an explosive wave. It was said that, at that time, nothing could stand against Cartesianism. This was no exaggeration, but solving the problem of man's identity was not to mean solving all the philosophical problems a great thinker like Descartes faced. It had a

---

[39] Iris Murdoch, *Metaphisics as a Guide to Morals* (Vintage, 2003), 437.

[40] Emmanuel Levinas, *Totality and Infinity* (1961), trans. Alphonso Lingis (Duquesne University Press, 1998), 211.

fundamental importance if he could explain this point that, despite all of our defects, imagining a being, which is the highest manifestation of the idea of perfection, of where it comes from.

Descartes could not give an acceptable answer to this question, one related to the values and was different from the problem of identity, in a similar way that he solved the problem of identity. Probably for Descartes, it was ideal if he could extract through the principles of geometry something related to perfection and completeness. In Greek tradition, the idea of perfection was entwined with circle, and circular movement was the most perfect form of movement. But by Kepler, almost all of those ideas simultaneously with the era of Descartes's youth were archived.

Descartes himself had founded analytical geometry, a system of coordinates by three axes perpendicular to each other that infinitely extended from three directions. What was the relation between infinity and perfection? How could he explain the idea of perfection with the system of coordinates in analytical geometry? This system of coordinates showed everything but numbers as redundant and additional. He could fit the whole thoughtless world in this system and explain the precise, clear, and distinct location of any trifling sand by the language of numbers. This system was a unique instrument for demystification of the world, but it could not solve Descartes's dilemma with respect to the concept of perfection.

The concept of natural orientation was in the repository of the prevailing concepts of the Middle Ages. According to that concept, God, for achieving sublime ends, had implanted this natural orientation in the inner nature of all beings he created. Adhering to that concept probably would not have been pleasing to Descartes. Accepting that was like granting an unwanted concession to the old concept of inclination and return of everything to its origin, which came from the philosophy of ancient Greece, especially an Aristotelian doctrine, and was blended with the teachings of the Middle Ages. With total enthusiasm, the young Descartes witnessed the abandonment of it for good by the ascension of the new Galilean mechanic. Now Descartes himself was a protagonist who had mocked such a concept.

There was a manipulated version of the idea of natural guidance or natural orientation, which was restricted to man in such a way that the outcome was interpreted as God's special gift for this thinking creature. The innate ideas was the byproduct of reason limited only to man and out of the reach of "simple machines" (solid) and "complicated machines" (animals). Descartes could easily locate the idea of a complete supreme being in this innate idea, but he did not. Why?

Descartes says,

> So because we find within ourselves the idea of a God, or a supremely perfect Being, we are able to investigate the cause which produces this idea in us; but after, on considering the immensity of the perfection it possesses, we are constrained to admit that we can consider it only as emanating from an all-perfect Being, that is, form a God who truly exists. For it is not only made manifest by the natural light that nothing can be the cause of nothing whatever, and that the more perfect cannot proceed from the less perfect . . . it is impossible for us to have any idea of anything whatever, if there is not within us or outside of us, an original, which as a matter of fact comprehends all the perfections.[41]

Imagining this embodiment of perfection was not an ordinary perception in Descartes's era in the same level of the other perceptions. Today, our attitude toward language is a playful one. We enter different language games and play in different fields like science, art, politics, and ethics. Today, our playful attitude is a fundamental obstacle in sympathizing with Descartes for understanding the problems he faced. We devalue the driving force and the hidden energy in terminology by bringing the word in the field of psychology and changing the type and rules of the game. We resolve it and do

---

[41]   Descartes, *Principles of Philosophy* (volume 1), 226.

this very innocently as well. This innocence, at least before the recent philosophical revolution, was justifiable.

Descartes asks where the concept of God as the greatest of all beings and a supremely perfect being that human thought is able to perceive comes from. Here, Descartes seeks the help of Middle Ages teachings. Based on those teachings, the thought of a weak and limited being, like man, cannot perceive an almighty and infinite being. Such reasoning inevitably reveals its power-orientedness. That is, Descartes's ontology is based only at the surface to the originality of thought, but in a close observation, it is a philosophy based on the originality of power, God's power. This is a fundamental power, and the whole creation is derived from that power. Descartes was saying something like that God has created the matter and move with his absolute supreme power and has maintained it with his predestined power.[42]

The consequence of this relying on God from the scientific point of view of that time is also interesting. According to Descartes, an atheist cannot reach to the certainty, so he cannot reach to a scientific knowledge:

> That an atheist can know clearly that the three angles of a triangle are equal to two right angles, I do not deny, I merely affirm that, on the other hand, such knowledge on his part can not constitute true science, because no knowledge that can be rendered doubtful should be called science. Since he is, as supposed, an Atheist, he can not be sure that he is not deceived in the things that seems most evident to him, as has been successfully shown; and though perchance the doubt does not occur to him, nevertheless it may come up, if he examine the matter, or

---

[42] M.J. Osler, *Divine Will and the Mechanical Philosophy* (Cambridge University Press, 1994), 123.

if another suggests it; he can never be safe from it unless
he first recognizes the existence of a God.[43]

These concepts, which Descartes use as an instrument in
establishing the dictatorship of reason, are the heritage of the Middle
Ages.

Maybe this very belief in the originality of power provoked
Descartes to neglect and negate the Aristotelian final causality.
Descartes believed we can't prove God's existence by saying that God
is the first cause. His power proves his existence. That is, even though
man's existence is based on his thought, the originality of thought
depends upon the existence of God, and the almighty power of God
proves the existence of God. When "I think therefore I am" reaches to
the level of God, it becomes "I exist because I am the supreme power."
Descartes's formula can then be summarized:

> I think. In my thought, there is an almighty supreme
> being. My thought per se cannot perceive an infinite being
> with a supreme power. Therefore, this infinitely powerful
> being exists, and it is he who causes his existence in my
> mind. This supreme perfect and powerful being is real
> (contrary to evil); therefore, he cannot be cunningly
> deceitful. Therefore, cunning and delusion cannot cause
> my being. Rather, it is a real being.

So by relying on this power, Descartes declares his famous
axiom. But this Cartesian starting point is also the beginning of
deconstruction of the framework of the precedence of major premise
over minor premise. Based on that framework, the minor premise,
which is "I think therefore I am," cannot be proven unless first the
major premise, which is "Everything that thinks exists" is proven.

---

[43]   Descartes, "Reply to Objections," in *The Philosophical Works*
(volume 2), 39.

Descartes, in *Meditations, Objections, and Replies,* has referred to this point.[44]

After the age of the discoverers of unknown lands, now it was the scientists' turn to discover the unknown realm of the matter. Thus, the age of dictatorship of reason began. But this dictatorship was quite different from the Church's dictatorship, which, at the time, was too weak to be able to harm against unbelievers. No one feared the Church's damnation any longer. The dictatorship of reason was dictated from reason itself. Inside every scientist and philosopher sat a dictator whose attitude toward the world had no basic difference from the attitude of a military commander:

"For myself, I have succeeded in discovering certain truths in the science . . . my encounter with these I look upon as so many battles in which I have had fortune on my side . . . to win more than two or three other victories."[45] Or "we might compare them to the Generals of our armies, whose force usually grow in proportion to their victories."[46] In the following piece, he analogizes the accumulation of scientific discoveries to the accumulation of wealth: "For it is much the same with those who little by little discover the truth in the sciences, as with those who, commencing to become rich, have less trouble in obtaining great acquisitions than they formerly experienced, when poorer, in arriving at those much smaller in amount."[47]

In the following piece, Descartes prefers the method of personal and authoritarian decision making of a rational person over the democratic public decision making. Though Descartes's verdict in special cases is correct, one must pay attention that he saw the application of this verdict very extensively and in no way accepted the tight and narrow limits we today determine for the validity of this verdict:

---

[44]   Ibid., 38.
[45]   Descartes, "Discourse on the Method," in *The Philosophical Works of Descartes* (volume 1), 123.
[46]   Ibid.,
[47]   Ibid., 122-123.

There is very often less perfection in works composed of several portions, and carried out by hands of various masters, than in those on which one individual alone has worked. Thus we see that buildings planned and carried out by one architect alone are usually more beautiful and better proportioned than those which many have tried to put in order and improve . . . those ancient cities which, originally mere villages, have become in the process of time great towns, are usually badly constructed in comparison with those which are regularly laid out on a plain by a surveyor who is free to follow his own ideas.[48]

Today, we have different aesthetics with respect to Descartes's time and see the old cities with intricate narrow alleys more beautiful than the straight, orderly, and geometrical new cities.

The above piece from Descartes shows that his cultural backgrounds were in contrast with the backgrounds of the contemporary democracies. Michael Walzer, who has brought the above piece in his article, "Philosophy and Democracy," says that the truth that he (Descartes) knows or claims to know is a unique truth; therefore, politics too has to be unique. Walzer adds that, of course, Descartes personally had no interest in the political narrative of the above way of thinking. Perhaps because he tended to remain the unchallenged ruler of his own mind.[49] Walzer says Descartes preferred to play the role of counselor whispering in the ear of power.[50]

Erasmus previously wrote, "The happiest status is reached when there is a prince whom everyone obeys, when the prince obeys the

---

[48] Descartes, "Discourse on the Method," in *The Philosophical Works of Descartes* (volume 1), 87-88.

[49] Michael Walzer, "Philosophy and Democracy," in *Debates in Contemporary Political Philosophy: An Anthology*, 363.

[50] Ibid., p. 362.

laws and when the laws answer to our ideals of honesty and equity."[51]
Q. Skinner eludes to the same thing in his article:

> However, by the rise of hereditary *signory* in the fourteenth
> century, this ... increasingly gave way to the claim that the
> best means of ensuring the good standing of any political
> community must be to institute the rule of a wise prince, a
> *pater patriae*, whose actions will be governed by a desire to
> foster the common good and hence the general happiness
> of all his subjects.[52]

MacIntyre, quoting from G. N. Figis, says that, immediately
after the Reformation, the absolute individual confronts the absolute
state.[53] Realities show that, at that time, they had absolutely a typical
image of an individual without any notice to his rights. This is a time
that the grounds for the emergence of the dictatorship of reason,
hand in hand with the authoritarian states, were prepared.

Today, the ground for accepting Descartes's ideas has declined, and
we may agree more with Hayek, the critic of the modern rationalism,
who says the ancient traditions that are realized during the centuries
in cities, buildings, institutions, social relations, values, and ethics
are the engraved product and gradual reforms of numerous peoples.
No individual or programming group can entirely do those things
whatsoever. Let us have a long quote from Hayek:

> It was mainly through him [Descartes] that the very term
> "reason" changed its meaning ... the new rationalism
> of Francis Bacon, Thomas Hobbes and particularly

---

51 Erasmus (1974:194), in Quentin Skinner, *The State* (1989) and
    Contemporary Political Philosophy: An Anthology, ed. R.E. Goodin and
    P. Pettit (Blackwell, 2002), 5.
52 Quentin Skinner, *The State* (1989) and *Contemporary Political
    Philosophy: An Anthology*, ed. R.E. Goodin and P. Pettit (Blackwell,
    2002), 6.
53 MacIntyre, *A Short History of Ethics*, 120.

Rene Descartes contended that all the useful human institutions were and ought to be deliberate creation of conscious reason ... it is a view which in the social sphere has since wrought immeasurable harm, whatever its great achievements in the sphere of technology may have been ... The ascendancy of this view in the seventeenth century implied in fact a relapse into an earlier naïve way of thinking, into a view which habitually assumed a personal inventor for all human institutions, be it language or writing, laws or morals. It is no accident that Cartesian rationalism was completely blind to the forces of historical evolution.[54]

Political Echo of Descartes's Philosophy

Toward the end of the seventeenth century, despite the fact that the Church was still powerful and the war of religions caused a lot of damage, European civilization stabilized overall. Industry grew; commerce blossomed. Grounds for propounding the theory of social contract as the theoretical struggle against the tyranny of kings were accommodated. The theory of social contract first came about for justifying the legitimacy of dictatorial states. Even though the precondition for the spread of this theory was the transition from the Cartesian reason toward a new understanding from nature, the genesis of the theory of social contract was impossible without the expansion and dissemination of one of the fundamental factors of Cartesian reason. This fundamental factor consisted of belief in that everything in our world and built by man, from cities to material objects to social relations, first is materialized, developed in a thoughtful mind, and then turned into reality by the will. Everyone accepted

---

[54] Fredrich Von Hayek, "Kinds of Rationalism," in *Studies in Philosophy Politics and Economics* (University of Chicago Press, 1967), 84-85.

this theory. Later, that is, from the eighteenth century and French Revolution and especially after the Romantic Movement and on, this belief turned into an effective tool serving the social revolutionary theories to such an extent that even Descartes could not dream it, and as it will be shown, he provided the cornerstone of the theory of total abandonment of the traditional beliefs (where they almost rebuked all the traditional beliefs with the label of superstition) and the destruction of the old social institutions and building of the new beliefs and social institutions (starting from zero). Paul Johnson, in *The Birth of the Modern World—Society: 1815-1830*,[55] describes one of the state-tailored modernization projects in Russia known with the name of Arachiev, which resulted in catastrophe.

It is a historical irony that how a conservative and discreet-minded philosopher like Descartes established such tenets that later served as a revolutionary instrument for political violence: "It seems to me that the best name for this kind of naïve rationalism is rationalist constructivism . . . It is from this kind of social rationalism or constructivism that all modern socialism, planning and totalitarianism derives."[56]

Ordinary Life in the Time of Descartes

Descartes never married. From the time of Aristotle until the age of Descartes and somehow until the twentieth century, ordinary daily life was not regarded in itself as something valuable. Life acquired meaningful and value while thinking on transcendental matters. The thought used for the welfare of family or amusement was not even considered as thought; it was wasting of time. The best work for a philosopher (who was definitely a male) was to avoid marriage and family life. A true thinker of that time believed that time spent on

---

55   Paul Johnson, *The Birth of the Modern World—Society: 1815-1830* (Harper Collins, 1991).
56   Fredrich Von Hayek, *Kinds of Rationalism*, 85.

companionship of the family was a waste. In that atmosphere, the man of philosophy believed that the company of his wife and family could be of no help to his salvation. Companionship and pastime within the family, especially with the children that today's consultants of family hygiene emphasize so much on and attribute the root of many family disorders to the lack of this basic necessity, were the great absence in the life of the elite, philosophers, scientists, and the rest until the few decades ago. By today's norm, it may seem that the ordinary uneducated people treated their own family much better and spent more time with them. It is true that, compared to the few thinkers and elites of that time, they spent more time with their family, but they deprecated this behavior of theirs. Anyway, they did not regard this act of theirs as something positive. We should also pay attention to this fact that most families until the nineteenth century not only were a social unit but also an economic unit as well. That is, women and children were workers whose fathers and succession of brothers were mostly their employers, and pastime in the household that we referred to in the above case was of the kind of worker-employer relation and void of content, like respect and care. If the philosophers of that time judge the value of today's life, the only valuable thing they would find in it is the period of research and education. Even they with more familiarity with today's goals of life, which, in most cases, do not accept any noble and superior goal other than this very life and its pleasures and conveniences, will take away any privilege that is given to education and researches of our time.

THREE

Nature as an Eternal
Huge Mechanism

Ideas and theories reveal a spectrum of interpretation when confronted with people with different interests and goals. But the same people reveal a consensus on their quasi-aesthetic attitudes as if they are in a state of collective trance.

> But if to be rational means to satisfy criteria, then this process of redefinition is bound to be non-rational. So if the humanities are to be viewed as rational activities, rationality will have to be thought of as something other than the satisfaction of criteria which are statable in advance.[57]

"Nature at that time does not refer to the existence of things but to the origin and foundation of truths."[58]

During the Middle Ages, believers saw nature as a place where its beauties were not true ones. They believed that the true beauties were in the other world, the eternal world. From the Renaissance on, nature was seen gradually as a beautiful place: "The Italians are the

---

57   Richard Rorty, *philosophical papers, volume 1*, 37.
58   Cassirer, *The Philosophy of Enlightenment*, 242.

first among modern peoples by whom the outward world seen and felt as something beautiful."[59]

From the sixteenth century on, two different trends gradually began to merge together: the immanent, sensible, and materialized beauty from one side and the intellectual and transcendental beauty from the other. The first trend was transforming a formerly not beautiful nature to a beautiful nature that was transforming the former pagan beauty/not true beauty to a secular and worldly beauty. The second intended to bring to our world the, up to that time, otherworldly eternal truth/beauty and eternalizing the secular world.

Descartes, by concentrating on a long-lasting Middle Ages package, constitutes an intermediate school between the traditional school and the modern Newtonian school by assimilating an originally eternal substance descended to the earth from paradise that is the thought/reason. He asserts that, not only our reason is the origin and reservoir of truth, but the driving force of our reason also is provided from its interior. According to Descartes, due to the divine origin of our reason, there is a potential that, if it is directed to the right path, it can recognize the truth from lies and good from evil. But according to Descartes, our feelings can darken and obscure our thought because our feelings are nurtured from our bodily desires. If we do not employ the correct way of thinking, we are always susceptible to face deviation from truth and fall into the trap of lies.

From Descartes in the seventeenth century to Newton in the eighteenth century, there are distinguished English philosophers, Hobbes and Locke. Here, a fundamental change takes place. Nature takes an enormous quasi-aesthetic attraction, not because, as we may say, it was now beautiful, but because they believed it was an immortal, huge mechanical system. And the laws of nature were the eternal mechanical laws. At that time, they admired the eternal mechanical systems and eternal mechanical laws both as the art facts of God.

---

[59]   Jacob Burckhardt, *Civilization of the Renaissance in Italy*, 152.

Nature now had turned into an attractive gigantic mechanism. Without this new quasi-aesthetic attitude toward nature, maybe the revolution in the natural sciences was not possible the way in which they took place. Today, we do not see any relation among mechanism, mechanics, mechanical relations, and aesthetic attraction, and it is ridiculous if one relates these two together. Today, mechanism and mechanical relations do not have the slightest aspect of quasi-aesthetic attraction. But in the seventeenth and eighteenth centuries, it was the other way around. The revolution in the attitude toward nature first occurred in England, and in fact, it was a different interpretation of nature, a revolution that summoned a phantom of ideas about nature ranging from the image of a lustful whore[60] craving to be raped by man up to a goddess to be worshipped.[61]

Contrary to the philosophy of Descartes, who took it for granted that our whole knowledge came from the inner source of our reason, now it was the goddess of nature who excited some feelings and impressions in the bodily senses of man, the feelings and impressions that were the unique source of all the data that accumulated to constitute man's knowledge and turn the so-called *Tabula rasa* into an active masculine subject who lustfully craved to manipulate the bodily limbs of the nature as a feminine object.

Here, we must pay attention to the great differences that separate our age from the seventeenth and eighteenth centuries. The desire to dominate nature at that time and the quasi-aesthetic attraction that was instigating this domination is totally strange to our time because

---

[60] Keith Thomas, *Religion & Decline of Magic* (1971) (New York: Charles Scribner's Son), 29. "In Aristotelian philosophy, what he . . . Jean-Baptist van Helmont (1579-1644) referred to in a striking phrase as the 'whorish appetite' of matter was given an active role in nature."

[61] Shaftesbury, "Hymn to Nature": "O glorious Nature! Supremely fair and sovereignly good! All-loving and all-lovely, all-divine! Whose looks are so becoming and of such infinite grace: whose study brings such wisdom, and whose contemplation such delight . . . O mighty Nature! Wise substitute of providence! Impowered creatress," in Ernest Cassirer, *Rousseau, Kant and Goethe*, trans. J. Gutmann, P. Oskar Kristeller, and J. H. Randal (Princeton University Press, 1970), 53.

it has been some decades that the horizontal respect goes forward to have a touch of quasi-aesthetic attraction while any attitude and behavior with a slightest touch of contempt gains a repulsive response.

With Hobbes and Locke, the place of truth is inside the nature, and the driving force of our thoughts does not come from its interior, but from our experiences, that is from our contact with the nature. By these contacts, some feelings are created in us that correspond with pleasure or pain. The driving forces of our thought are these very factors of pain and pleasure: "*Delight* or *uneasiness,* one or other of them join themselves to almost all our ideas, both of sensation and reflection: and there is scarce any affection of our senses from without, any retired thought of our mind within, which is not able to produce in us *pleasure* or *pain.*"[62]

How did the inward, thought-oriented attitude in Descartes transfer to the outward, nature-oriented attitude in Hobbes, Locke, and Newton? And where did the source of the energy necessary for this transfer was supplied from? Now the word "nature" as the eternal source and origin of all the eternal truths was full of energy and had the same weight, credibility, and unique attraction that thought had for Descartes. The great force, which in Cartesian philosophy was incarnated in the word "thought/reason," now was inside the word "nature." This new paradigm brought its own consequences, the negation of the innate ideas in man and viewing the state of mind of a newborn child as a *Tabula rasa.*

Now the source of truths was transferred from the interior of thought to the inner core of nature. This was a decisive separation from the Cartesian doctrine and a complete breaking off from the concepts of the Middle Ages. If Descartes viewed thought as the source and reservoir of all known truths up to that time and the truths that must be known after that, now the truths lied in the reservoir of nature. Since that time, the most basic measure of credibility of every

---

[62] John Locke, *An Essay Concerning Human Understanding,* ed. Roger Woolhouse (Penguin Books, 1997), 129.

theory that claims the truth was by returning to nature. Although for both, the materialist Hobbes as well as the idealist Locke, the origin of all of our ideas goes back to nature, passing from Hobbes to Locke, a god is seen that expresses itself through nature.

From the end of the seventeenth century and throughout the eighteenth century in Europe, the word "nature" seemed as if newly discovered. Now "nature" was radiating with full energy. If we put the pagan views in parentheses, nature by its Middle Ages Christian connotation was a valueless, mortal creature and in contrast with the eternity of the other world. The attitude that Descartes had toward nature did not lead to Locke's attitude toward nature. We do not find a linear and constant transformation from the first to the second. In the Cartesian paradigm, all important data exudes from the reservoir of reason. But in physics and in nature, the application of reason was producing remarkable results. Mechanics, mechanism, and whatever was named as the industry of man were becoming attractive. The mechanical interpretation of nature actually prepared the nature for research. This was what Cartesian school also was prepared to conform to. The depths of nature were like a lock whose key was the man's reason. "Yet most of those who conceived of the universe as a great clock were in practice slow to face up to the full implications of their analogy."[63]

A totally different picture of nature emerged from the end of the seventeenth century. The picture that celestial mechanics was rendering from cosmos now acquired an unprecedented attraction. Thus, the orderly and lawful depths of nature were hiding an inaccessible truth that was only surrendered to reason, the excavator, which, in a superior place, epitomized in the philosopher, which meant more to the scientist and researcher at that time and was far from its old meaning.

But the newly discovered nature of the modern philosophers, especially the English ones, had unknown depths, which, at that

---

[63]   Keith Thomas, *Religion & Decline of Magic*, 80.

depth, eternally fixed laws of nature were at work. Richard Rorty writes about this:

> The idea that rational enquiry should make visible a realm to which non-intellectuals have little access, and of whose very existence they may be doubtful. In the Enlightenment, this notion became concrete in the adoption of the Newtonian physical scientist as a model of the intellectual. To most thinkers of the eighteenth century, it seemed clear that the access to nature which physical science had provided should now be followed by the establishment of social, political, and economic institution which were in accordance with nature.[64]

This was a nature far from the access of ordinary people, far from divulging its inner secrets to anyone other than the man of reason. Therefore, what was exposed as the phenomenon was not regarded real, but its interior was real, and the truth could only be found in its secrecy.

For Locke, truth was a brilliant word, like a shining sun. Discovering eternal and universal truths were the most important goal of life for the scientific elite of that time. The words like "truth" had deep and majestic values that remained untouched until the twentieth century. Today, we are amazed on why they played so much with these words at that time. At the time of Locke, words like "truth" and "reality" still maintained their Middle Ages attractiveness. In the Middle Ages, words like "truthful" and "real" were not used to mean "real and tangible" the way we understand these words. Because the assumption was that God, eternity, and the other world are real, and truth could only be found in relation with them. But the material and tangible things were not real; they were void of truth. At the time of Locke, when words like "truth" and "real" were used for nature, all the

---

[64]   Richard Rorty, *Objectivity, Relativism and Truth—Philosophical Papers* (volume 1) (Cambridge University Press, 2005), 22.

energy, value, and attractiveness of these words were transferred into the word "nature" and "natural." Now every truth and every real thing were seen in relation with nature and matter instead of being seen in relation with the other world or God. This new approach to nature had such an amazing and unexpected consequence that separated the modern age from the Middle Ages in an irreversible way. With this attitude, Descartes is a mediator philosopher who has prepared the way for dissolution of the beliefs of the Middle Ages. When we separate from the premodern era, we are following Descartes, but when we enter the modern world, we are following Locke. The modern world does not begin with the Cartesian attitude but with Locke's attitude toward nature and man.

> Following the age of Luther and Machiavelli, we should expect the rise of a kind of moral-cum-political theory in which the individual is the ultimate social unit, power the ultimate concern, God an increasingly irrelevant but still inexpugnable being, and a pre-political, pre-social timeless human nature the background of changing social forms.[65]

Man's nature, like nature despite the diversity and capriciousness of appearance, had in its depth an unchangeable and eternal order that was accessible only to a philosopher who would methodically explore it with patience. What is important here (and at least was prevalent in England) is the similarity of the research methods about nature and man's nature. Charles Taylor writes about this: "The goal of a naturalist account of man comes in the wake of the scientific revolution of the seventeenth century. It is the aim of explaining human beings like other objects in nature."[66]

The people of an era, who initiated to the new attitude toward nature with its new content and meaning out of their interest, will,

---

[65]   MacIntyre, *A Short History of Ethics*, 125.

[66]   Charles Taylor, "The Diversity of Goods," in *Philosophical Papers* (volume 2), 242.

and consciousness, did not know what its consequences was in the long run. Through this attitude, natural law emerged as an ideology and questioned the traditional right of sovereignty of the kings. In the question, which in its consequence, the king was seen as the usurper of power.

When nature emerged as the eternally ordered mechanism, why were all of the political factions initiated to this new attitude and absorbed by its consequences? Why were the people of those times, from monarchy to the opponents of autocracy, attracted toward it? It is reasonable to accept that the new attitude absorbed the opponents of tyranny, but why monarchists and supporters of tyranny?

We may think that the age of the benevolent dictator kings was over because now, after a century after the war of religions, there was no need for a shield against the Church. Now that they had fortified a suitable freedom of research and thought, such that the Church no longer could operate like the time of Galileo, they had to surrender their privileges. Or we may think that the new social forces had emerged and the economic structure was changed. That is why the bourgeoisie as a class were expanded, and now they were craving for the political power.

I think these views simply neglect the notion of the quasi-aesthetic attraction of certain words in certain spheres, which we can check them as the incarnation of the long-lasting attitudes, which are independent from the interest, will, and consciousness of the people who live that paradigm. Thus, the responsive attitude to the attraction of words is neither propounded in aesthetics, philosophy, nor politics. That is simply ignored. These kinds of questions are examined only in their indirect and transformed way in moral philosophy, and again, what is not paid attention to are the quasi-aesthetic attraction of certain words and their amazing transformations in different spheres or spaces.

> Attitudes are distinguished by rupturing from each other, and in the beginning they emerge as frustration from the previous attitude and a weak tendency to a new attitude. Those things that were attractive no longer mean much.

On the contrary, those things that were not prevalent before, or they were limited to a few, suddenly are welcomed by many. In the beginning, a new attitude, do not show a tendency for being theorized, and at this stage, they appear credible and harmless and that's why they often ride through theoretical and social barriers without facing a serious obstacle. But when the new attitude was theorized, it render's a totally different composition and suddenly appear as a deep rift.[67]

This quasi-aesthetic specificity leads the different and even contradictory social caucuses and classes to merge in a wonderful consensus. The new naturalism of the seventeenth century was a change of times and a great transformation in outlooks. The nature, which now was being emphasized on, was the basis of foregrounds of all changes. This new naturalism extended to the whole continent, and it was a far-reaching development in the "demystification" of the world in the Weberian lexicon.

This was a new paradigm. Normally, in a new paradigm, a cluster of words, which now have a close relation with each other, gain quasi-aesthetic attraction and are regarded as strong values as if they have lots of energy. Sometimes, new words are generated to name them, and sometimes, old words, while keeping the old and traditional meaning, find new meanings that are attractive and full of energy. Meanwhile, some acquire a spectrum of vast meanings. Remember the word "reason" in Descartes's era, which acquired a vast spectrum of meaning including virtue, peace, salvation, reverence, and so forth. Today, in our time, there is no consensus about those meanings. The word "nature" too, when it became a symbol for a wonderful, huge, eternal mechanism and gained a quasi-aesthetic dimension, its spectrum of meaning also expanded in a blended form. Charles Taylor says the meaning of the word "nature" changed during the seventeenth century. "On the old outlook, the nature of something

---

[67]   Bahman Bazargani, (*The Matrix of Beauty*), 221-222.

is the idea it instantiates. The modern is more ready to identify the 'nature' of the thing with the forces or factors which make it function as it does, and this can no longer be seen as existing independently of the particulars which function this way. Nature is within."[68]

Lukacs also lists three different meaning for nature for this period:

> Thus the word "nature" becomes highly ambiguous. We have already drawn attention to the idea, formulated most lucidly by Kant but essentially unchanged since Kepler and Galileo, of nature as the "aggregate of systems of the laws" governing what happens. Parallel to this conception . . . there is another conception of nature, *a value concept*, wholly different from the first one and embracing a wholly different cluster of meaning . . . At the same time if one thinks of Rousseau, there are echoes of a quite different meaning wholly incompatible with this one . . . And with a reversal of meanings that never becomes apparent, nature becomes the repository of all these inner reification. Nature thereby acquires the meaning of what has grown organically, what was not created by man, in contrast to the artificial structures of human civilization. But, at the same time, it can be understood as that aspect of human inwardness which has remained natural, or at least tends or belongs to become natural once more. "They are what we once were," says Schiller of the forms of nature, "they are what we should once more become." But here, unexpectedly and indissolubly bound up with the other meanings, we discover a third conception of nature, one in which we can clearly discern the ideal and the tendency to overcome the problems of a reified existence. "Nature" here refers to authentic humanity, the

---

[68]   C. Taylor, "Legitimation Crisis," in *Philosophical Papers 2*, 257.

true essence of man liberated from the false, mechanizing society.[69]

Cassirer also states this blending of the different meaning of nature:

> The concept and the word "Nature" in the thought of the seventeenth century embrace two groups of problems, which we today usually distinguish from one another, and include them in a single unit ... "Nature" at that time does not refer to the existence of things but to the origin and foundation of truths.[70]

Nature in general and human nature in particular now was the realm of emerging values that were previously assumed to be as a gift from God. Locke's analogy of man to a *Tabula rasa* actually meant the rejection of the "innate ideas" of man that lasted centuries and yet was prevailing in Descartes's philosophy.

What Locke meant of "reason" and "nature" was not the same with that of Descartes's. The problems that Locke was confronted with and the points he emphasized on and attended to were different with Descartes's problems:

> Rationalism has existed at widely different times and in the most diverse forms . . . But there are fundamental distinctions to be made, depending on the *material* on which this rationalism is brought to bear and on the *role* assigned to it in the comprehensive system of human knowledge and human objectives.[71]

---

[69] George Lukacs, *History and Class Consciousness*, trans. Rodney Livingstone (London: Merlin Press, 1971), 136.

[70] Cassirer, *The Philosophy of Enlightenment*, 242.

[71] George Lukacs, *History and Class Consciousness*, 113.

If we do not notice the importance of the quasi-aesthetic attitude of the people living in a paradigm, we may conclude that there is a power of provocation in the books, that is, the ideas and theories in them. But why a book/idea that is revolutionary in one paradigm is not provocative in another paradigm? Here, we should attend to the quasi-aesthetic tendencies and biases of the people living in an era. Because it is based on these tendencies and biases that this or that attitude is formed, consequently, this or that theory is chosen like a useful tool.

Perhaps that is the reason why the ideas and theories that were operating in an era to justify the sovereignty of rule change into rebellious and subversive ideas and theories in another era, as it were for the idea of social contract. If we take Grotius as the founder of the theory of natural law, Hobbes too is the first founder of the idea of social contract, and certainly we cannot label ideas Hobbes stated in *Leviathan* as a rebellion against despotism of the kings. But the post-Hobbes's ideas, especially those of Rousseau's, changed the idea of social contract into a revolutionary one.

Even though Hobbes justifies an absolute power in what today we call an omnipotent and repressive state, he nonetheless is the founder of a different school in Western political philosophy whose view is distinct from the Cartesian view of political power. In the introduction to *Leviathan*, C. B. Macpherson writes:

> He [Hobbes] exposed the lineaments of power more clearly than anyone had done since Machiavelli, more systematically than anyone had ever done, and than most have done since[72] . . . and convents, without the Sword, are but Words, and of no strength to secure a man at all. Therefore notwithstanding the Laws of Nature . . . if there be no Power erected, or not great enough for our security; every man will and may lawfully on his own strength and

---

[72]   C.B. Macpherson, "Introduction to *Leviathan*" (Penguin Books, 1985), 9.

art, for caution against all other men[73] . . . the only way to erect such a Common Power, as may be able to defend them from the invasion of Foreigners, and the injuries of one another, and thereby to secure them in such sort . . . is, to confer all their power and strength upon one Man, or upon one Assembly of men, that may reduce all their wills, by plurality of voices, unto one Will.[74]

All versions of the theories of social contract are based on the free and isolated individual, like atoms, living next to each other. Their relation to each other is subjected to the concept of scarcity/ abundance of the material sources of their environment. So there is either constant war or constant peace. Hobbes's version is constant war. "Every man is enemy to every man." Rousseau's version is based on the "noble wild" living in peace. The emergence of the ideas of the social contract as a consequence of this kind of individualization was impossible without the destruction of the remaining subjective structures of the Middle Ages and the authority of God and the Church and the emergence of the new authority based on the originality and authority of nature.

But the notable point in here is that the school of materialism, which also was the result of originality and authority of nature, did not pay much attention to the rights and freedom of these individuals. Most of the materialist philosophers, such as Hobbes and later Holbach and LaMettrie, were determinists. The attention of the materialist school of the eighteenth century was not toward rights of man but for opposition to the Church and Christianity. What they meant of liberty was liberty from church and Christianity, and if an atheist dictatorial rule would have been founded on the basis of their materialistic ideas, it would have been likely that they would have preferred it over the states that favored liberty and advocated religious tolerance. In this outlook, the hard-line natural laws guided

---

[73]   Thomas Hobbes, *Leviathan* (Penguin Books, 1985), 223-224.
[74]   Ibid., 227.

the nature and man. In the nineteenth century, "the same attitude was pointedly expressed by August Comte, who asked 'if we do not allow free thinking in chemistry or biology, why should we allow it in morals or politics?'"[75]

Anyway, this materialism couldn't help to nurture ideas about liberty. This assistance came from the side of the thinkers who were not materialists. While most of these thinkers totally accepted the originality of nature and its independence from God, they believed in a man who was responsible for his actions vis-à-vis God. These thinkers, when compared with their materialist and atheist counterparts, cared a lot for man's rights and liberties. According to Hobbes, an individual is compared to an atom that only cares for the tangible force and power; therefore, he incarcerates him in the bondage of a dictatorship based on the contract. Locke's proprietor is responsible before God and is expected to care for morals, so he should have his individual rights. Like Machiavelli, Hobbes did not care for the religious sentiments. The differences between Hobbes and Locke were the differences in their starting points and the relevant principles. Unlike Locke, Hobbes did not see a god, which was supposed to be the source of benevolence at that time.

Most of today's political philosophers extol Hobbes and identify him as the first founder of the idea of social contract. But Hobbes's version of social contract, unlike Locke's, has nothing to do with liberty. Hobbes's pessimist concept of man has close kinship with the Christian concept of man's original sin. If Christianity appeals to God for controlling the bodily desires and emphasizing piety, Hobbes, for ending the dispute emanating from the men's needs and desires, establishes the absolute power of the state (*Leviathan*). The idealistic concept of Locke, despite his faith in God, deconstructs the Christian concept of man's original sin and offers a different interpretation of the nature of man, an interpretation that prepares the way for the concept of liberty.

---

[75] Isaiah Berlin, "Two Concepts of Liberty," in *Four Essays on Liberty* (Oxford University Press, 1969), 151.

Hobbes's picture of man is without any transcendental side. Man is a domineering animal who craves power to satisfy his needs and desires. Because power is the only guarantee to satisfy his needs and desires, the more power, the better it is. Thus, in Hobbes's picture of man, there is no limit or bound for this desire of power. C. B. Macpherson has developed and showed this point very well that the Hobbes's model of man is a bourgeois involved in the market. Just as the commodities exchange in the function of the market, Hobbes's man too is involved in the breathtaking exchange of power.[76]

Although Hobbes's concept of freedom is now quite vivid among the other concepts of freedom in political philosophy, it was not a favorite concept during three centuries after Hobbes. For a long time, the concepts of Locke and Rousseau of liberty pushed aside Hobbes's concept of liberty. In that period, Locke's theory, which was a moral theory, plus the revolutionary theory of Rousseau were much more favorite concepts of freedom. Kant completed Rousseau's concepts, but from the nineteenth century on, problems emerged, and the divergent, even opposing, concepts of liberty stood face to face. We may remember what liberalism and communism meant of liberty. As the author mentioned it before, according to Charles Taylor, freedom by Hobbes is freedom of movement in three directions. That is, freedom has nothing to do with salvation or moral progress.

But the way that Hobbes opened had great consequences. The interpretation of man's nature by emphasis on Galilean outlook took the principle of constant motion in place of the Middle Ages principle of status quo. The amazing result that is obtained from this outlook was the emergence of the idea of equilibrium, which was not the result of status quo, but equilibrium based on the balance of powers. Newton used this principle in interpreting the motion of globs. This principle was not limited to nature, but to the nature of man, which was seen as an equilibrium, which was coming from the

---

[76] C.B. Macpherson, "The Theory of Human Nature in Society," In *Reading Political Philosophy*, ed. N. Warburton, J. Pike, and D. Matraverse (London: Routledge, 2000), 100-105.

balance of incompatible powers. This outlook freed certain structure of the nomenclatures, which were banned during the Middle Ages. Unlike the Middle Ages and even the time of Descartes, it was no longer possible to divide the desires into sublime and shoddy. Now the desires were seen as forces, which the equilibrium of human nature came from their balance. Forces for change could use the tools that were banned or discredited against the traditional forces.

This new attitude to man's nature opened the way for the deconstruction of sublimity, which was characteristic of the Middle Ages. Desires were freed from the hoop of dos and don'ts and changed to physical forces, which the equilibrium of human nature was from their competition. All of those new achievements, whether in physics, celestial mechanics, or in the nature of man and psychology, was the result of a new attitude toward the movement and balance of forces, an attitude that was the harbinger of the emergence of a different paradigm.

FOUR

THE CONCEPT OF BALANCE

Alexander Pope said, "Nature and Nature's laws lay hid in night, God said:'let Newton be,' and all was light."[77]

The Middle Ages was the period of belief in noble values. But at the dawn of the modern world, a surface-oriented attitude replaced the sky/heaven-oriented attitude of the Middle Ages. The fifteenth and sixteenth centuries were the era of discoverers of the continents and unknown lands. People were infatuated with exploring the surfaces. But this trend did not last long, and the monistic discourse of thriving rationalism suppressed the somehow pluralistic discourse of humanism.

With the beginning of the Age of Reason, a different trend emerged, which lasted in the realm of art until the emergence of impressionism and in the realm of philosophy until Wittgenstein's Tractatus. From then on, it was assumed that truth and credibility was originating from depths, and an irresistible urge for deep bathymetry sat in the eyes. Words like "deep" and "profound" became attractive and eye-catching. Within more than three centuries, attentions and concentrations focused on the depth of matter and nature. So, words like "depth" and "deep" acquired a transcendent quality. Kant also placed the noumenon far away from the access in the depths, and if the irresistible attraction of bathymetry did not exist, it was not known whether Freud could supply the wonderful realm of unconscious.

---

[77]   Cassirer, *The Philosophy of Enlightenment*, 44.

In the seventeenth century, "Truly 'philosophical' knowledge had seemed attainable only when thought, starting from a highest being and from a highest intuitively grasped certainty,"[78] but "It [the eighteenth century] seeks another concept of truth and philosophy[79] . . . The attempt to solve the central problem of philosophic method involves recourse to Newton's *Rules of Philosophizing* rather than to Descartes's *Discourse on Method* with the result that philosophy presently takes an entirely new direction."[80]

Unlike Ernest Cassirer's perception, this entirely new direction was impossible without preparing the related backgrounds. Cassirer, like many other academics, believed in scientific revolution as the consequence of sudden emergence of a new theory. But new theory is the product of the new structure of nomenclatures, and these too are the product of the new attitude. So when the new attitude toward nature developed (and I confess that I have clumsily dealt with it in chapter three and without enough research), we confront with the new structure of nomenclatures that emphasize on the words like "matter," "depth," and "feeling." These words were the hot points full of energy. They replaced the old structure of nomenclatures that were emphasizing on the words like "soul," "heaven," and "above." These latter words were now cold points bereft of energy, and they seemed to be void of truth, credibility, and attraction. Also, the old method of research, which was oriented from the absolute to the conditional and from above to below and from general to particular, changed to an experimental method with a new orientation, that is, from below to above and from particular to general. From Descartes to Newton, what changed was the attitude that irreversibly altered the old orientation.

In the old astronomy, the stars were fixed to the spheres, and it was with revolving spheres that stars revolved. But by the time of Galileo, the old theory of cosmos had lost its validity. With the

---

[78]   Ibid., 6.
[79]   Ibid., 7
[80]   Ibid.

Copernican revolution, the centrality of Earth became a legend. Even before Galileo, the old belief in existence of spheres too did not have credible supporters. Therefore, the stars were freed from the bond of Ptolemy's spheres and changed into masses that were in constant motion in their orbits. Now, there were some problems that must be answered. If there were no spheres, then where was the driving force of the revolving globes supplied from? The answer that Galileo gave was straightforward and simple. Galileo suggested that, if we change our attitude, we will not see any problem, that is, we should take motion as the permanent state and search for the cause of status quo. The universe that Galileo perceived was a world in which motion was a permanent state and status quo was a temporary state. This was a new paradigm totally different from the old one. Now there was no need to explain the motion of stars. Galileo's response solved a problem, but there were other problems because the answers that were credible and acceptable in the old paradigm now had lost their credibility. The problems that made the old order helpless were solved, but the problems that had acceptable answers in the old order now had no reasonable answer for them in the new order. Galileo had discovered the laws of falling bodies, but unlike the Aristotelian paradigm, there were no reason for the acceleration of the falling heavy bodies. The old order attributed the cause of the falling heavy bodies to the natural tendency of heavy bodies in reaching the center of the Earth, and in this belief, the more weight a body has, the more velocity will be its fall. Galileo proved that, if one can eliminate the friction of the air, the velocity of the falling cotton or plume will be equal with the falling stone or lead. This was an amazing discovery that totally disarmed the Aristotelian paradigm. But Galileo's mechanic did not have much to say about the source of the acceleration of the falling bodies. It was clear that an increasing force was exerting on a falling body, but Galileo's principles did not explain this force. In the new system, especially from Galileo and Descartes, bodies and matters were perceived as bodies that only had extension. So the solid bodies could not have any tendency, desire, or will, as it was in the Aristotelian paradigm. Anyone who attributed a tendency or desire to matter and body was confronted with grin and sarcasm. When Newton (1642-1727) offered his gravitational force, he attributed a tendency or desire to matter, which, a few decades before him, Descartes not only refuted the existence of any desire or tendency with sarcasm but characteristics like scent and color in the matter as well. If such a negative label wouldn't have been marked on desire or tendency, maybe the theory of gravity would have emerged sooner.

Anyway, gravity was interpreted not as a tendency or desire, but as a force and power. The Aristotelian theory was saying that a tendency in massive bodies pulls them toward the center of the Earth. Newton's theory called this tendency "force" and attributed it both to the falling stone and the Earth. If Earth, due to its massive weight was pulling the stone with great force toward itself, then the stone too was pulling the Earth by a weak force toward itself respectively. Obviously, this was not possible before Copernicus. Newtonian science introduced some kind of relativity in relation to motion. Now, force and motion were relative factors. A universe with stationary and absolute poles of heaven/Earth became a world with relative motions and balancing of forces. So the previous absolute authorities now could be relative authorities. This was a real earthquake. Newton's laws of gravity not only explained the cause of the movement of stars and elliptical orbits but also the cause for the fall of an apple and its falling curve and its velocity. By Newton's gravitational theory, the remaining theories of the old world were completely abandoned.

Newton's theory explained the constant motion of the celestial globes as balance and equilibrium between gravitational and centrifugal forces. Therefore, wherever there was a constant circular motion according to Newton's model, there must have been balance between two opposing forces. When Hobbes before Newton saw man's thoughts, desires, and needs as their constant motion inside the body of man, he used Galileo's theory of constant motion in explaining man's unending desires and wants. Now that Newtonian paradigm had stolen the show, the theory of balance of powers was finding a proper ground such that it expanded and entered the realm of society and politics.

In the new paradigm, nature was seen as the balance between natural powers, and human nature was seen as the balance between human desires respectively. We may follow Macpherson's interpretation, in his introduction to *Leviathan*, that the picture of a universe with a god who rules over the world from above and the picture of society as king, prince, and lord who rules over the masses of people was substituted by the theory of balance of powers that was based on the market model. The theory of the balance of powers provided a suitable foundation for the genesis of the theory of balance of political powers that was formulated by Montesquieu and later became the main structure of democratic society.

Now the sordid, bodily desires that were reproached from the time of the stoics and especially perceived as the reason for the fall and decay of man in the Middle Ages were attended to with a different outlook. "The passions were now pronounced to be invigorating rather than pernicious."[81]

The study of human nature, his feelings, and ideals, which began with Locke, was pursued with more power and intensity:

> It sounds like a violent revolution when Vauvenargues, in his *Introduction to the Knowledge of the Human Mind* (1746), says that the true nature of man does not lie in reason, but in the passions. The Stoic demand for control of the passions by reason is and always will be a mere dream . . . Voltaire says in his *Treatise on Metaphysics* that without the passions, without the desire for fame, without ambition and vanity, no progress of humanity, no refinement of taste and no improvement of the arts and sciences is thinkable . . . And Diderot's . . . *Philosophical Thoughts'* begins similarly with this idea.[82]

---

[81] Hirschman, *The Passions and the Interests*, 10-11.
[82] Cassirer, *The Philosophy of Enlightenment*, 107.

Now, man's body was no longer the ebullient root of sins, so the bodily desires too were not wicked. This meant as the deconstruction of moral values: "This astounding transformation of the moral and ideological scene erupts quite suddenly, and the historical and psychological reasons for it are still not wholly understood."[83]

With the Age of Reason and beginning of the three centuries of discipline and order, Foucault's narrative from the formation of the modern world, some of these bodily desires were seen as opposed desires. Now the opposed desires control each other: "In elaborating his theory of the passions in the *Ethics*, Spinoza puts forth two propositions that are essential for the development of his argument: 'An affect cannot be restrained nor removed unless by an opposed and stronger affect.'"[84]

Hirschman shows the theory of controlling the bodily desires was widespread at that time:

> And the same language is found in the more elaborate formulation of d'Holbach: The passions are the true counterweights of the passions; we must not at all attempt to destroy them, but rather try to direct them: let us offset those that are harmful by those that are useful to society. Reason . . . is nothing but the act of choosing those passions which we must follow for the sake of our happiness.[85]

It seems that this thesis did not last long and whatever was told by the thinkers who lived at that time necessarily was not happening. In the next chapter, we will see that, by the emergence of liberty, once more, many of the old moral values superseded over the bodily desires and suppressed them. What happened and took place was neither in concordance with the predictions of the major philosophers of that

---

[83]   Hirschman, *The Passions and the Interests*, 11.
[84]   Ibid., 23.
[85]   Ibid., 27.

time nor the emphasis of the ideals of their Christian opponents who were terribly hoping that the Christian values be erected.

In the seventeenth century, monetary relations expanded, every kind of material wealth found a common criterion in the body of money, and everything was capable of being exchanged and measured with it. Let us quote from Foucault:

> Wealth becomes whatever is the object of needs and desires; it is split into elements that can be substituted for one another by the interplay of the coinage that signifies them; and the reciprocal relations of money and wealth are established in the form of circulation and exchange . . . it was the universal instrument for the analysis and representation of wealth, because it covered the entire extent of its domain leaving no residuum. All wealth is *coinable*; and it is by this means that it enters into *circulation*—in the same way that any natural being was *characterizable*, and could thereby find its place in a *taxonomy*; that any individual was *nameable* and could find its place in an *articulated language*; that any representation was *signifiable* and could find its place, in order to be *known*, in a *system of identities and differences*.[86]

The economy/profit-oriented tendencies jointed with minimizing the expenditure for the well-being were regarded as some kind of virtue from the sixteenth century, especially since Luther:

> If one were to ask them what is the aim of their restless chase and why they are never satisfied with what they have acquired . . . they would answer, if they had an answer at all . . . that business, with its ceaseless work, had quite simply become "indispensable to their life." That is in fact their only true motivation, and it expresses at the same

---

[86] M. Foucault, *The Order of Things* (1966) (London: Routledge, 2004), 190.

time the irrational element of this way of conducting one's life, whereby a man exists for his business not vice versa.[87]

Thus, a bourgeois who was restlessly after profit was regarded as a reasonable man and his deeds and thoughts "clear and distinct" and hence predictable. We must pay attention that, after Descartes, words like "clear" and "distinct" had such a credibility that must have been considered and observed from the side of anyone who claimed being reasonable and knowledgeable. Based on this teaching, we can clearly[88] and distinctively recognize the causes and incentives of the thoughts and deeds of a greedy person. But if someone were after thrill, glory, name, and dignity, he could at any moment engage in an activity that was in contradiction with his material interests. The thoughts and deeds of such a person were not predictable, and the connection between them and his interests were not clear and distinct. Such a person could be found more among the nobles and royal courts at that time than among the middle class. It was only after the emergence of the Romantic Movement that spontaneity and unpredictability once more emerged as the attractive characteristics of the romantic man who was stealing the scene, those characteristics that are still under the attention of the modern art.

There was much talk, from the late seventeenth century on, about the *douceur* of commerce. The most influential exponent of the doctrine of the *doux commerce* was Montesquieu. In the part of *Esprit des lois* that deals with economic matters he states in the opening chapter: "It is

---

87   Max Weber, *Protestant Ethics and Spirit of Capitalism*, 23

88   Principle XLV, "I term clear which is present and apparent to an attentive mind … But the distinct is that which is so precise and different from all other objects that it contains within itself nothing but what is clear." (Rene Descartes, "Principles of Philosophy, Principle XLV," in *The Philosophical Works of Descartes* (volume 1), trans. Elizabeth S. Haldane, C.H., LL.D., G.R.T. Ross, M.A., and D. Phil, 237.

almost a general rule that wherever the ways of man are gentle (*moeurs douces*) there is commerce; and wherever there is commerce, there the ways of men are gentle." And later in the same chapter he repeats: "Commerce . . . polishes and softens (*adoucit*) barbarian ways as we can see every day."[89] Twenty one years after the publication of Montesquieu's work the just cited phrase is found almost verbatim in the work of the Scottish historian William Robertson, who writes in his *View of the Progress of Society in Europe* (1769): Commerce tends to wear off those prejudices which maintain distinctions and animosity between nations. It *softens* and *polishes* the manners of men.[90]

The belief in trade as an inherently peaceful and peacekeeping activity that was parallel with the theory of the balance of forces lasted until the French Revolution. But again, contrary to the prediction of the philosophers of the Enlightenment and contrary to the way Hirshman's interpretation is going, from the French Revolution and on, the direction of the evaluation of war and peace changed. War was not for the sake of trade but for the sake of liberty, which now had an irresistible quasi-aesthetic attraction, became a sacred ideal. Liberty now was evaluated as the true essence of humanity that romantics, liberals, and religious and nonreligious people were carrying its flag. Thus, the idea of the balance of powers that originally was an English idea left the scene. With the French Revolution, the teachings of Locke on liberty was faded and hollowed while the teachings of Rousseau on the general will and communal liberty came to the scene.

———⚜———

The new concept of nature with its eternal laws operating in the depths led to the emergence of a spectrum of new ideas that, on one

---

[89]   Hirschman, *The Passions and the Interests*, 59-60.
[90]   Ibid., 60-61.

extreme, was the deism with a hope for a united, refined, and scientific natural religion to unite the whole modern world away from its old religious divisions. And on the other extreme, a refined, tolerant God had nothing to do after the Genesis. Thus, a new belief formed in which man could penetrate into the depths of nature and identify its coherent and eternal laws by acting on them. Consequently, one could step on the way to enlightenment, happiness, and fortune. Therefore, a scientist who labored toward the discovery of the laws of nature was a man who not only worked toward the discovery and understanding of the hidden will of God, but by this work, he directed the humanity from darkness toward lightness and knowledge.

The sense of deep contentment that scientists of that period felt from their research and the immense sense of morality that accumulated in them were taking all its energy from the science as a member of the team of the words that had a quasi-aesthetic attraction at that time. That was a feeling that scientists of the twentieth century never touched its threshold because reason and science were drained from virtue and beauty and changed into an instrumental reason. Not that we would have two kinds of reason, but when reason was bereft of its quasi-aesthetic attraction, it was nothing other than an instrumental reason. The difference between these two reasons comes from the differences of paradigms. During the Age of Reason, reason was attractive. It was seen as reason overflowed with moral senses as virtue, good, benevolence, peacefulness, and so forth.

Pre-Romantic Moral Revolution

We observed that the bodily senses changed into the source of credibility. It was within such a condition that a general belief emerged as if the only credible moral authority to evaluate our deeds is that "particular faculty," that is, "a sixth sense," that one feels within herself. According to this concept, if I could listen to this sense such that my acts and behaviors become in concordance or close to that, I could take steps toward the perfection of my personality. Georgio Agamben writes about the emergence of the idea of the point of perfection:

> Around the middle of the seventeenth century the figure
> of the *man of taste* makes its appearance in European
> society: the figure, that is, of the man who is endowed
> with a particular faculty, almost with a sixth sense, as they
> started to say then, which allows him to grasp the *point de
> perfection* that is characteristic of every work of art.[91]

To excel the personality meant I can exploit as maximally as
possible from my faculties. One who could turn this particular faculty
from potential to de facto meant that he himself has approached the
point of perfection. In the traditional moral of premodern world,
the above question was never asked because the idea of making the
maximum of our inner hidden talents essentially comes from the
modern world. In the premodern world, the question was how is it
possible to become a good, moral, and, in general, as similar to an
ideal, perfect man?

The concept of the ideal perfect man was formed in the Middle
Ages. The behavior based on the commandments of the Holy Book
provided the framework of this ideal. The pious who lived in the
convents provided solid tradition for this ethic. Even though this
moral perfect man was no longer attractive since the Renaissance,
when it came to reckoning, it was reasonable. With Luther's teachings,
this ideal perfect man had become much more prudent. Middle-class
prudence had a different side, and that was prudence in moral matters.
The ideal perfect man was a reasonable and prudent man, and the
more reasonable he was, the more prudent he was. By acting based
on an ideal that was supposedly the ideal of the Holy Book, he would
become the man whom God was supposed to reward in the world
and afterlife. Within two centuries, from Luther to Diderot, and by
the quasi-aesthetic revolution that placed the nature and eventually
the human nature in place of God, step by step, vast changes took
place in moral grounds such that the model of an ideal moral man

---

[91]   Giorgio Agamben, *Man Without Content* (1994), trans. Georgia Albert
(Stanford University Press, 1999), 13.

who listened to his inner sense was different in every aspect from the old perfect man. This was a fundamental transformation in morals and a change in the inner of man, without which the emergence of the Romantic Era and a temperament or nature, which since then was labeled as "romantic," was difficult to picture. Following this transformation, the old criterion of reason changed as well. If it were supposed that a man who was to be reasonable after his salvation, then the modern man who was after the voice of his inner sense either was not reasonable or, if he were supposed to be reasonable, his criterion of reason was different from the criterion of the reason of a devout Christian. William Blake, who was painting the devil as a young, beautiful rebel, maybe had these as a background. With this background, one must go after Rousseau and understand his hatred from the consequences of corruption of civilization, which, according to him, "led to hypocrisy and falsehood." Rousseau believed that civilization had closed our eyes and ears and corrupted us and prevented us from paying attention to our inner sense.

FIVE

MY FREEDOM OR OUR
SALVATION?

It seems that one cannot explain the complexities of the contemporary world by relying on any monistic outlook. Every one of the outlooks had whirled in this field, and the result is a collection of outlooks whichever one, in turn, had played a role in weaving this texture. An outlook that plays a deterrent role and is supposedly after deconstructing the social or political texture in one period seems to change its attitude in another period and help with for its continuation and consolidation. Therefore, we have no choice other than accepting a pluralistic outlook.

In this chapter, I have meditated on the negative side of Rousseau's political ideas, and it may seem as though I intended to confer that Rousseau had a share in the crimes against humanity that took place by the modern totalitarian states in the twentieth century. As it is mentioned before, I consider the theories as the tools produced by the thinkers. They do it in the same manner that an artist, for example, a painter, does it usually without knowing the outcome of her work. Both artist and thinker are deeply attracted and absorbed by their themes and their sketches as well as their materials. So we should deal with Rousseau and Nietzsche the same way we deal with Wagner and Dali. The point is not to judge on the thinkers or the artists. Rather, it is to hesitate on the quasi-aesthetic attraction effect that was focused on certain ideas during the modern time.

With the French Revolution, Rousseau's ideas became the ideas of revolution, and no attention was given to Locke's moderate ideas.

Hence that kind of attitude toward life, which is labeled as the specificity of English version of liberty after Hayek, was paid less attention to. We can say that, during the two centuries that bridge the French Revolution to the breakup of the Soviet Union, the attraction of revolutionary Rousseau could not be comparable with Locke, Mill, Constant, and others. Hayek believes there are incongruous impressions of liberty: the revolutionary French impression and the liberal English impression. In an article titled *Freedom, Reason, and Tradition*, he emphasized the difference between the French and English understanding of liberty. Due to its importance, let us read some long quotes from him:

> Though freedom is not a state of nature but an artifact of civilization, it did not arise from design. The institutions of freedom, like everything freedom has created, were not established because people foresaw the benefits they would bring. But, once its advantages were recognized, men began to perfect and extend the reign of freedom and, for that purpose, to inquire how a free society worked. This development of a theory of liberty took place mainly in the eighteenth century. It began in two countries, England and France. The first of these knew liberty; the second did not. As a result, we have had to the present day two different traditions in the theory of liberty: one empirical and unsystematic, the other speculative and rationalistic. The first based on an interpretation of tradition and institutions which had spontaneously grown up and were but imperfectly understood, the second aiming at the construction of a utopia, which has often been tried but never successfully. Nevertheless, it has been the rationalist, plausible, and apparently logical argument of the French tradition, with its flattering assumptions about the unlimited powers of human reason that has progressively gained influence, while the less articulate and less explicit

tradition of English freedom has been on the decline.[92] This difference was better understood a hundred years ago than it is today. In the year of the European revolutions in which the two traditions merged, the contrast between "Anglican" and "Galician" liberty was clearly described by an eminent German-American political philosopher. "Galician liberty," wrote Francis Lieber in 1848, "is sought in the *government*, and according to an Anglican point of view, it is looked for in a wrong place, where it can not be found . . . the French look for the highest degree of political civilization in organization, that is, in the highest degree of interference by public power."[93] The greatest difference between the two views, however, is in their respective ideas about the role of traditions and the value of all the other products of unconscious growth proceeding throughout the ages.[94]

Continuing on, quoting from Talmon, Hayek writes about these two different schools: "One stands for organic, slow, half-conscious growth, the other for doctrinaire deliberateness; one for trial and error procedure, the other for an enforced solely valid pattern."[95] And Hayek himself concludes as this: "In this respect the British philosophers laid the foundations of a profound and essentially valid theory, while the rationalist school was simply and completely wrong."[96]

It can be said that, from the point of view of the philosophers like Richard Rorty, in the last sentence we quoted from Hayek, the "foundations of a profound and essentially valid theory" probably has some problem. In his *Philosophical Papers* (Volume 1), Rorty recurrently confessed his debt to Dewey and Davidson in saying that

---

[92] Friedrich Von Hayek, *The Constitution of Liberty* (University of Chicago Press, 1961), 54-55.

[93] Ibid., 55.

[94] Ibid., 61.

[95] Ibid., 56.

[96] Ibid., 125.

validity or nonvalidity of a theory, instead of being an unhistorical or abstract truth, depends on the changing preconditions without which not a single agreement about anything could be obtained.

Hayek there continues, "The sweeping success of the political doctrines that stem from the French tradition is probably due to their great appeal to humane pride and ambition."[97] It is not clear why those teachings now do not exult in our soul. Have we lost our "feeling of pride and ambition" today? We may attention to the fact that, at the time of Hayek, the word "reason" had lost its supreme position in the team of words that had a quasi-aesthetic attraction at the time of Descartes and hence had left many of its previous implicit meanings like good, virtue, fairness, tolerance, and tendency for peace. We should note that, in the writings of Descartes's era, the word "reason" generally had these positive specificities. At that time, it seemed they were inherent in reason. Because Hayek belongs to a tradition in which there is no room for the attraction or emptiness of words, despite his own celebrated insight, he does not consider these specificities of words. That tradition had captured his mind to such a degree that, again, he unwillingly and perhaps not deliberately devaluates himself and his colleagues in a period:

> It seems to be true that it is on the whole the more active, intelligent, and original men among the intellectuals who most frequently incline towards socialism, while its opponents are often of an inferior caliber . . . the most brilliant and successful teachers are today more likely than not to be socialists, while those who hold more conservative political views are as frequently mediocrities. This is of course by itself an important factor leading the younger generation into the socialist camp.[98]

---

[97] Hayek, *The Constitution of Liberty*, 56.

[98] Hayek, "The Intellectuals and Socialism," in *Studies in Philosophy Politics and Economics* (University of Chicago Press, 1967), 188.

Neither today's holders of the conservative political views are more talented and wiser than their leftist counterparts; nor were the Marxist thinkers of those years more talented and wiser than their conservative counterparts. These kinds of arbitrations belong to the mistakes that the quasi-aesthetic field of attraction of the time impacted. The academic tradition, which Hayek too, like many of his sympathizers as well as his opponents, belongs to, does not see the deep fault that opens in the middle of the attraction and emptiness of words and fails to review the quasi-aesthetic attraction of Nicole Kidman, Leonardo DiCaprio, and Diego Maradona of today; Pablo Picasso, Salvador Dali, and others of yesterday; and Isaac Newton, Rene Descartes, and Galileo Galilei, in preyesteryears as the same phenomenon.

Locke: Emphasis on the Individual Liberty

It is true that modern political philosophy with its apprehension about security begins with Hobbes, but modern political philosophy with its apprehension about securing individual rights, mistrust toward state, and effort to limit its power begins with Locke. In fact, after Locke, political philosophy realizes the individual rights. In Locke's view, unlike Hobbes's, liberty has an inseparable bond with private property:

> Locke's thought brings to the fore a theme absent or denied in the thought of Hobbes and Spinoza—the theme of the links between the right to personal property and individual liberty. There is in Locke what is lacking in earlier individualist writers—a clear perception that personal independence presupposes private property, securely protected under the rule of law. After Locke, the claim that a civil society demands the widespread diffusion of personal property becomes a staple theme

of liberal writing, and it is this insight which embodies
Locke's greatest contribution to liberalism.[99]

Liberty, at that time, seemed as a possibility in relation with
private property. For Locke, it was not easy to accept that a time
would come that liberty not only would be independent from the
private property, but nearly for a century all over the world, a great
part of the intelligentsia believe in the abolition of private property as
the most important provision for "liberty."

The association of private property and liberty was the result of
the social conditions of that period:

> Servants and beggars (who in the seventeenth century
> were probably more than half the male population of
> England)[100] . . . At the start of the eighteenth century,
> more than half of the population [of England] lived on
> the margins of subsistence. The masses were not only
> largely illiterate but also so pauperized that they could
> not even pay for literature. They did not have at their
> disposal the buying power needed for even the most
> modest participation in the market of cultural goods.[101]

So, liberty was not in direct link with what the poor people of that
period were waiting for. Owing to Charles Dickens, we have a clear
image of poor people in the England of nineteenth century. We find
the fear from the right of the poor people to vote and the danger of
the majority to pressure over minority, even near John Stuart Mill:

---

[99] John Gray, *Liberalism (Concepts in Social Thought)* (Minneapolis: University of Minnesota Press, 1986), 12-13.

[100] MacIntyre, *A Short History of Ethics* (1967), 148.

[101] Jurgen Habermas, *The Structural Transformation of the Public Sphere*, trans. Thomas Burger and Frederick Lawrence (Cambridge: MIT Press, 1989), 37-38.

But now Mill saw the inevitable extension of the principle, and that the "numerical majority" . . . and Mill . . . saw also what he took to be the dangers of extensions: in particular, a tyranny of opinion and prejudice—the "will of the majority" overriding and perhaps suppressing minority opinion. When Mill came to write his essay *On Liberty*, the emphasis had shifted and Mill had moved with his times. The central concern, now, was with the preservation of the rights of individuals and minorities, against Public Opinion and the democratic State. And it was here that he found Coleridge so useful to him, particularly Coleridge's idea of the "clerisy"—a nationally endowed class, "for the cultivation, and for diffusing its results among the community . . . We consider the definitive establishment of this fundamental principle to be one of the permanent benefits which political science owes to the Conservative philosophers.[102]

Locke's emphasis on the private property as a guarantee for the individual liberty and Mill's emphasis on protecting individual rights and the fear from the majority's dictatorship was not unwarranted: "Bismark kept its plebiscitary-conservative consequences in mind when he included the universal franchise first in the constitution of the North German Federation, then . . ."[103]

The consequence of the association of liberty and property as the interwoven and inseparable rights was the association of the virtue and reason with liberty. But the important point was that the private property was regarded as a material factor to generate and to guard liberty. This interpretation of liberty regarded owners of private properties as avant-garde of liberty.

---

[102] Raymond Williams, *Culture & Society: 1780-1950* (New York: Columbia University Press, 1983), 56.

[103] Jurgen Habermas, *The Structural Transformation of the Public Sphere*, 145.

From sixteenth century on, economic activity, especially trade, worked as a tranquilizer of the war-ridden society of the Europe of that time and was glorified from the spirit of middle class in contrast with the spirit of warmongering and pride-seeking nobility and royalty of Europe. The era of pride and chivalry ended and Cervantes—with an eye in which alas and pity were woven together—created Don Quixote. "It was Karl Marx who remarked that what Don Quixote had to learn was that not every economic order is equally compatible with knight errantry."[104] Hannah Arendt too emphasizes on the association of private property and liberty at that time: "To the eighteenth century, as to the seventeenth before it and the nineteenth after it, the function of laws was not primarily to guarantee liberties but to protect property; it was property, and not the law as such, that guaranteed freedom."[105]

In the opposite of Locke, it is in Rousseau that the fundamentalist liberty found its great thinker. Below, some of the political doctrines of Rousseau are reviewed with criticism, but it does not mean that his positive doctrines are ignored.

Rousseau: Liberty as a Revolutionary Calling

Unlike Locke, who saw liberty as individual liberty and regarded it as the epiphany of private property, the liberty that Rousseau realized is collective liberty. Rousseau showed a great deal of sensitivity toward social inequalities and considered property as the main factor for inequality and was ready to sacrifice the private property for the public property. Rousseau's model was Sparta, and the general will that Rousseau emphasized was similar to the Spartan's public will that appeared in public gatherings with the thunder they bellowed from their throat expressing their positive or negative vote. The importance of Rousseau is largely due to the deep impact of his

---

[104] MacIntyre, *A Short History of Ethics*, 144.
[105] Hannah Arendt, *On Revolution*, 180.

doctrine over the revolutionaries of the eighteenth century and on. They regarded Rousseau very close to their political ideals. Rousseau can be justifiably named as the first thinker of the modern age revolutions whose theories had many commonalities with totalitarian states that were supposed to bring not only Europe but a great part of the world under their thumb:

> In order then that the social compact may not be an empty formula, it tacitly includes the undertaking, which alone can give force to the rest, that whoever refuses to obey the general will shall be compelled to do so by the whole body. This means nothing less than that he will be forced to be free; for this is the condition which, by giving each citizen to his country, secures him against all personal dependence. In this lies the key to the working of the political machine;[106] Each of us puts his person and all his power in common under the supreme direction of the general will, and, in our corporate capacity, we receive each member as an indivisible part of the whole.[107]

The generations who came after the Age of Enlightenment and on enthusiastically welcomed a world that had much more association with Rousseau than Locke. What a penalty they paid for it. Charles Taylor writes about this: "The immense gap between the atomist and general will theories is thus clear. What the second sees as a defining feature of the degenerate case is understood by the first as a structural feature of all societies."[108]

We should pay attention to Rousseau's subject:

> Again, the Sovereign, being formed wholly of individuals who compose it, neither has nor can have any interest

---

[106] Rousseau, *Social Contract*, chapter seven (book one).

[107] Ibid., chapter six (book one).

[108] Charles Taylor, "Social Theory as Practice," in *Philosophy and the Human Sciences—Philosophical Papers* (volume 2), 100.

contrary to theirs; and consequently the sovereign power need give no guarantee to its subjects, because it is impossible for the body to wish to hurt all its members. We shall also see later on that it cannot hurt any in particular. The Sovereign, merely by virtue of what it is, is always what it should be. This, however, is not the case with the relation of the subjects to the Sovereign, which, despite the common interest, would have no security that they would fulfill their undertakings, unless it found means to assure itself of their fidelity.[109]

In continuation, Rousseau implicitly attacks Montesquieu and explicitly attacks the separation of powers as legislative and executive, the result of the balance of powers:

But our political theorists, unable to divide Sovereignty in principal, divide it according to its object: into force and will; into legislative power and executive power . . . Sometimes they confuse all these sections, and sometimes they distinguish them; they turn the Sovereign into a fantastic being composed of several connected pieces: it is as if they were making man of several bodies . . . We are told that the jugglers of Japan dismember a child before the eyes of the spectators; then they throw all the members into the air one after another, and the child falls down alive and whole.[110]

Because Sparta had not rival parties and trade unions, the prescription that Rousseau wrapped for the modern society is similar:

It is therefore essential, if the general will is to be able to express itself, that there should be no partial society

---

[109] Rousseau, *Social Contract*, chapter seven (book one).
[110] Ibid., chapter two (book two).

within the State, and that each citizen should think only his own thoughts . . . But if there are partial societies, it is best to have as many as possible and to prevent them from being unequal, as was done by Solon, Numa, Servius. These precautions are the only ones that can guarantee that the general will shall be always enlightened, and that the people shall in no way deceive itself.[111]

Rousseau makes the power of the state so absolute that it can even baffle Hobbes. The limits of Hobbes's *Leviathan* were the life and property of the individuals. In Hobbes's theory, the reason for the existence of the state was to protect the life and property of the individual while the state of Rousseau claims the individual's life as well as his property for the service of all. Rousseau says it is the duty of the state to exploit every individual and maximize his faculties [for all] to the highest possible degree. This is Luther's teachings about the unequivocal duties of a Christian plus a totalitarian state whose most important duty is to oversee in reaching the maximum exploitation from individual facilities for general elevation.

Rousseau's concept of society is a utopia that is a single and solid organization without any kind of suborganizations like trade unions, which he takes them as weak points. Rousseau's utopia is a Leviathan without a society. It is a society that is totally changed into a single and seamless organism. If Hobbes would have come to life and seen Rousseau's Leviathan, he truly would have been petrified from this modern monster and of the future world that Hobbes looked hopefully to. But most of the revolutionaries, which during two centuries after Rousseau saw their utopia and ideal in founding an organic society through the Rousseau-ian Leviathan, either put their head under the guillotine or lost their lives in the gulags. Rousseau also predicted this and saw it as a profitable deal for the individual:

---

[111]   Ibid., chapter three (book two).

It is seen to be so untrue that there is, in the social contract, any real renunciation on the part of the individuals, that the position in which they find themselves as a result of contract is really preferable to that in which they were before. Instead of renunciation, they have made an advantageous exchange: instead of an uncertain and precarious way of living they have got one that is better and more secure; instead of natural independence they have got liberty, instead of power to harm others security for themselves, and instead of their strength, which other might overcome, a right which social union makes invincible. Their very life, which they have devoted to the State, is by it constantly protected; and when they risk it in the State's defense, what more are they doing than giving back what they have received from it?[112] Furthermore, the citizen is no longer the judge of the dangers to which the law desires him to expose himself; and when the prince says to him: "It is expedient for the State that you die," he ought to die, because it is only on that condition that he has been living in security up to the present, and because his life is no longer a mere bounty of nature, but a gift made conditionally by the State.[113]

The final chapters of *Social Contract* are not less worrying:

How can a blind multitude, which often does not know what it wills, because it rarely knows what is good for it, carry out for itself so great and difficult an enterprise as a system of legislation? . . . The individuals see the good they reject; the public wills the good it does not see. All stand equally in need of guidance. The former must be compelled to bring their wills into conformity with their

---

112   Ibid., chapter four (book two).
113   Ibid., chapter five (book two).

reason; the latter must be taught to know what it wills . . . This makes a legislator necessary.[114]

> In order to discover the rules of society best suited to nations, a superior intelligence beholding all the passions of men without experiencing any of them would be needed . . . He who dares to undertake the making of a people's institutions ought to feel himself capable, so to speak, of changing human nature, of transforming each individual, who is by himself a complete and solitary whole, into part of a greater whole . . . He must, in a word, `take away from man his own resources and give him instead new ones alien to him, and incapable of being made use of without the help of other men. The more completely these natural resources are annihilated, the greater and the more lasting are those which he acquires, and the more stable and perfect the new institutions; so that if each citizen is nothing and can do nothing without the rest.[115]

Unlike today's prevailing procedures, Rousseau does not see legislation as the right of people and their representatives but devolves this important task to one man with perfect wisdom and addresses the ordinary people with obscene words. Of course at that time, such contemptuous discourses were not limited to Rousseau. The democratic procedure that is somehow prevalent today is not the result of Rousseau-ian outlook, and it is not the result of the Cartesian, even Kantian school of reason because they all believed that a superman thinker must show the right way to the demos. This superman thinker/philosopher would discover the principles. Then these principles were taught by professors to pupils and ordinary people: "For someone, as a philosopher, has to go to the first grounds

---

114 Ibid., chapter six (book two).
115 Ibid., chapter seven (book two).

of this concept of duty, since otherwise neither certitude nor purity can be expected anywhere in the doctrine of virtue."[116]

It was generally accepted that, without a philosopher, we could not touch the truth in the depth and hence the purity and trustfulness that accompanied it. Only the work of philosopher helped to crystallize the pure principles by detecting the impurities in order to reach purity and certainty. To reach purity and to gain trust as its consequence, a philosopher should perform a series of filtering operations. One of the common filtering operations was to determine which thoughts and deeds were related to feeling and which ones to reason, and anything that was determined to be negative or positive, "sensual" or "rational," would be labeled accordingly. But the philosopher would not totally discard what he had labeled as "sensual." The one labeled "sensual" could only be used when it was sponsored or controlled by "reason."

"If we cease to think of reason as a source of authority, and think of it simply as the process of reaching agreement by persuasion, then the standard Platonic and Kantian dichotomy of reason and feeling begins to fade away. That dichotomy can be replaced by a continuum of degrees of overlap of beliefs and desires."[117]

Among other important filters were the ones relating words like "temporary/permanent" and "volatile/durable." Whatever labeled temporary and volatile was valued as negative; whatever labeled permanent and durable was valued as positive. One of the characteristics of these filtering was the circular effect (changing cause to effect and vice versa). Often what was labeled as unstable/ stable, they considered it to be related to sense/reason, respectively. If we pay attention to these criteria of stability/instability, we easily would accept that whatever is related to the sense would be regarded as temporary and unstable and all the same repetitive. This very

---

[116] Immanuel Kant, "Metaphysical First Principles of the Doctrine of Virtue," in *Practical Philosophy*, trans. and ed. Mary J. Gregor (Cambridge University Press, 1999), 509-510.

[117] Richard Rorty, *Philosophical Papers* (volume 4) (Cambridge University Press, 2007), 53.

phenomenon of being temporary, unstable, and repetitious can also be observed on whatever that is related to reason. But because the philosopher has labeled the brand of "stable" on the reason, we easily, as if we have been hypnotized, accept that, yes, they are stable. In fact, so long as we take the mind as a room whose landlord is reason and its tenant is sense or so long as we take it as a property of a lord in which reason is lord and sense is subject, this kind of reasoning seems reasonable and convincing. But if we take the mind as a radio/television's broadcasting studio that is in the occupation of different performers at different hours, then, observe reason and sense as the serial occupiers or performers of this room, then try to forget that until this very yesterday, we used to see reason as the elite and the sense as the commoner, yes, it is only in this situation that the results of all those filtering, which no longer work in today's practice and experiment for a long time and do not attract our attention, also lose their credibility in the realm of theory. This kind of structure of the nomenclatures too will disappear like the lost attraction of the philosophers.

Why Rousseau Wins

Why did Rousseau's doctrines surpass Locke's doctrines? What kind of a strange essence did Rousseau's doctrines have, which fascinated the world for two centuries? Today, when we look back, we wonder how, even after Rousseau intellectual thinkers like Constant and Mill, were sidestepped and the rebellious utopias of Rousseau became the expression of passionate revolutionaries.

Yes, theories by themselves are not important. A theory is automatically brought under the attention when its reasoning, logic, and structures that it emphasizes on has a share in building the identity of that field of attraction. They nurture and get their energy from our quasi-aesthetic attitudes. Only after the emergence of these attitudes does the theories that are congruent with them attract attention, seem reasonable, and are introduced by many credible sources. As a result, they find many readers, and the theories that are incongruous with them seem irrational and unreal or simply hollow and unrelated to our problems. Consequently, they are abandoned. In other words, the reasonability of a theory in a paradigm and emptiness and meaninglessness of that theory in another paradigm would bring us to this conclusion that the evaluation of this or that theory from the point of view of their rationality/irrationality cannot pass from the walls of that paradigm. Reasonableness of a theory is the judgment of a paradigm in which a theory is produced in or has come under the attention. In the history of thought occasionally, we observe that a theory that has been forgotten for long suddenly has been discovered by the emergence of new attitudes and welcomed just as a diamond that was hidden in the sand and grit for a long time.

It can be said that a new call came with the French Revolution. It was as if seraphim had blown into his trumpet. A fundamentalist perception of liberty started that had generic similarities with the vertical and upward-oriented liberty of the Middle Ages. That unity of mankind as an ideal and the monistic attitude that the religions had fought for creating one world with one religion for more than a millennium and at last they all tired and reconciled with the reality of a pluralist world, although this was a very limited kind of pluralism, now revived again with a secular ideal. With the emergence of the fundamentalist perception of liberty, this understanding was reached that, once more, the world is on the way to unity. A new era of instabilities and callings—and ideals in a nonreligious form this time—began.

From the second half of the nineteenth century with the expansion of socialist ideas and the emergence of Marxism and its development during the twentieth century, a new fundamentalist perception of freedom emerged, liberation from the domination of the private property. Within the communist parties, the idea of individual freedom was discarded as a bourgeois slogan and was waned in the brilliant attraction of the fundamental liberation of humanity from the yoke of exploitation of capital and private property. Based on this idea, the abolition of private property was gradually leading to the establishment of a classless society, waning and abolition of the class tyranny and state's repression, and, ultimately, the emergence of the real and fundamental liberation of man.

Today when we look at the past, it seems, as if for the international communist movement, equality in comparison to liberty had been a more important aim. Such an outlook hides the immense energy and the quasi-aesthetic attraction that incorporated the idea of liberty. Liberty was an Archimedean stand around, which a consensus was established out of the interest, will, and consciousness of the people living that era. The quasi-aesthetic attraction of liberty was the necessary precondition for the slogans as "liberty from the yoke of private property and exploitation of capital" to be accepted by many of the revolutionaries and thinkers as well as a vast number of people. This precondition paved the way for this kind of slogan to be seen as rational and credible. The highest and most supreme aim of the global wave of the international communist movement was not equality in enjoyment of material blessing. There is no doubt that the idea of equality was not only a target but also an expected consequence of the leftist movements. But the idea of equality did not play a major role in supplying the enthusiasm and the driving force that moved them. A great part of this remarkable driving force was supplied from the energy reservoir that "liberty" was liberating.

The interesting thing in here is that, despite the negative impact that socialism had on individual liberties, socialism with tearing and discarding the umbilical cord that grafted the liberty with private property, created a new condition. This was a historic separation[118] that was destined to last at least a century so it could result in the separation of the two meanings of liberty, as negative liberty and positive liberty, as Berlin developed it.

Virtue is an equivocal word that, in each paradigm, incites or invokes conducts and discourses that are close to the strong values. For example, when they used the word "virtue" in the Middle Ages,

---

[118] The theory of grafting individual freedom with the right of private property on one hand and the theory of grafting democracy with the market on the other hand after the breakup of the socialist camp again flourished.

normally they meant a cluster of highly valued behavior and the kind of thoughts that supposedly accompanied a true believer of God. In the time of Descartes, virtue included reason that is a cluster of the highly revered behavior and thought of the time. And finally, it was associated with the liberty in the recent centuries and never separated from it. Hand-to-hand new values came into existence with new meanings of virtue, and with the Romantic Movement, these values distanced from reason. Thus for the first time after more than two thousand years, reason and virtue, which were intertwined since the time of Plato, separated from each other, and it did not take long that reason was named the instrumental reason. But the virtue—thus separated from reason and separated from private property with the spread of the Marxist wave—was not left alone. Now, virtue joined liberty, and the meaning of virtue since then merged in the act of political struggle, which supposedly elevated the militant individual to a level above the daily life. This was to mean the deconstruction of ancient virtue and formation of the new virtue. John Elster reminds that the sublime and attractive aspect of the political activity was especially noticed by John Stuart Mill:

> He saw political activity not only as a means to self-improvement, but also as a source of satisfaction and thus a good in itself. As noted by Albert Hirschman,[119] this implies that "the benefit of collective action for an individual is not the difference between the hoped-for result and the effort furnished by him or her, but the some of these two magnitudes."[120]

When we pay attention to the role and importance of virtue with the above meaning, then the understanding of the great driving force that Marxism achieved with swallowing the virtue as the

---

[119]   A. Hirschman, *Shifting Involvements* (Princeton University Press, 1982), 82.

[120]   J. Elster, "The Market and the Forum—Three Varieties of Political Theory" (1986), in *Contemporary Political Philosophy* (Blackwell, 1997), 138.

sibling of the modern political activity becomes easier. Lenin later would supply the theory of the avant-garde party, the driving force of virtue would provide a moral meaning for the professional militants and revolutionaries, and a professional revolutionary activist will be the new man associated with the new virtue and intended for overthrowing oppressive and unscientific old order and establishing the new order.

For Locke, freedom meant individual's liberty. But after the French Revolution, liberty became the sacred aim of life, and a fundamentalist liberty prevailed over the English impression of liberty. Now life itself was not the goal, but liberty was the goal of life. And the struggle for liberty became sacred, just as sacred that Christian faith was in the Middle Ages. The result of the above development was weakening of English understanding of liberty as individual liberty and strengthening of "French understanding from liberty"[121] as a revolutionary calling. These two understandings of liberty were the two sides of the fault line that Isaiah Berlin later will emphasize and warned by separating the negative liberty from positive liberty. Those crystallized values and beliefs in the revolutionary calling provided the fuel for the violence throughout the twentieth century and ultimately after the breaking up of the Soviet Union and socialist bloc suddenly welted among the seculars.

But after the breakup of the socialist block, there was an important turnaround in the field of quasi-aesthetic attraction. Liberty definitively left the quasi-aesthetic attraction, which had occupied it for two centuries. During this period, liberty merged with the power structure and got a hegemonic stand there. Liberty gave up its quasi-aesthetic attraction because a new field of quasi-aesthetic attraction was being formed.

Presently, there are two totally different impressions of liberty. The first is a fundamental impression from liberty that has become

---

[121]   If we take the countries of northern Europe, we have to say that this was a continental impression that France was the most prominent model of it and, of course in France itself, also were philosophers who were closer to English impression and vice versa.

the ideological cover of the new conservatives and feeds the aggressive strategy of the warmongers who are not far from the power. The second impression of liberty is based on the mutual respect between different outlooks and cultures. This is not a self-determined liberty. Rather, it is liberty for choosing different lifestyles.

Prior to the conquest of enlightenment and its universal principles, different lifestyles were operating in the forms of rural life in every place. These lifestyles that were the signs of practical pluralism in the premodern era before the Age of Enlightenment were regarded as the natural lifestyles of rural life. With enlightenment came the universal principles that knew only one kind of "reasonable" and "correct" lifestyle, decried other lifestyles, and condemned them to annihilation. The modern state, which Rousseau's general will more or less inspired:

> [L]ed inevitably to further weakening of the localized mechanisms of reproduction of previously autonomous ways of life; such mechanisms appeared to central power as so many obstacles on the way to the kind of society it projected, given its tendency to uniform administrative principals. Differences between ways of life were correspondingly redefined as relations of active mutual engagement. Popular, locally administrated ways of life were now constituted, from the perspective of universalistic ambitions, as retrograde and backward looking, a residue of a different social order to be left behind; as imperfect, immature stages in an overall line of development toward a "true" and universal way of life, exemplified by the hegemonic elite; as grounded in superstition or error, passion-ridden, infested with animal drives, and otherwise resisting the ennobling influence of the truly human—shortly to be dued "enlightened"—order. Such a redefinition placed the elite, for the first time, in a position of a collective teacher on top of its traditional role as the collective ruler. Diversity of ways of life has become now a temporary phenomenon, a transient phase

to be left behind in the effort aimed towards a universal humanity . . . On the whole, the inferiority of other forms of life, and the range of those of their aspects to which the judgment of inferiority was applied, were a function of the judging power's ambitions—their scope and administrative skills to back them . . . The aspects of human life now picked up for conscious regulation came to be known as "culture."[122]

At first, it seemed that different lifestyles would be transmuted in a single reasonable and scientific lifestyle of modernity. But this in practice did not happen. Consequently with the breakup of the socialist bloc, liberty lost its universal attraction. Now the pluralistic lifestyles also turned the modernity into a variety of small spaces of different lifestyles, religions, and cultures that now could no longer be suppressed. Two hundred years of the domination of liberty as a long narrative, in Lyotard's words, had led to the suppression of freedom of different lifestyles.

After the French Revolution, the intelligentsia had a conviction that the application of reason's principles could lead to the fixation of a reasonable lifestyle as the only right and good way of life. So they did not accept the pluralistic lifestyles of today. What they considered as liberty was a human calling that especially turned into the sacred goal of the individuals as well as nations. The assumption was that everyone had the same impression of liberty or they should have. Thus essentially, a vertical and fundamentalist liberty was constituted, which was the most primal epiphany of man's life. This liberty was based on a monistic reason. That is, the assumption was that reason has a single criterion. The conclusion drawn from this monistic reason and its universals was important. They too infused cohesive and homogenous criterion for individual character, lifestyles, morality, and ethics. This monistic reason was a major obstacle for choosing different lifestyles and moral criterion.

---

[122] Sigmond Bauman, *Intimations of Post-Modernity*, 7-8.

Thus, the fundamentalist liberty in the realm of action ran into an inextricable contradiction.

As we shall see in the next chapter, Berlin, in opposition to the doctrines like Rousseau's, divides liberty into two parts, the positive and the negative. He cuts the relation of reason with liberty, which, in the classical rationality, was interwoven together in that way. We know that, from Descartes's time, the human reason replaced celestial reason (logos), but all the same, the very virtue that was included in the logos and was guiding man toward salvation still was kept and included in the new one. Berlin's emphasis on the negative liberty is a step-by-step disarming of the classical reason and transition to a pluralist condition that reason has lost its former sacred nimbus and been turned into the instrumental reason. The preassumption of classical rationality was this that the reasonable man, by relying on reason, would have this internal power that can get on a general and universal road.

Today, when we look at the past, it seems it was clear at that time that different people would be choosing different lifestyles. The differences of these lifestyles are based on the difference of their tendencies. But this is our today's judgment, and we are not under the influence of the field of quasi-aesthetic attraction of that time. Today, we take the individual differences for granted and know that choosing this or that lifestyle depends on this or that inner tendency in us. But in the past, the universalistic impression of reason imposed universalistic impression of liberty. If the criterion of reason were one for all people, the impression from liberty must have been one. Therefore, only one lifestyle and one system of moral values, responsibilities, and duties that resulted from it was reasonable. It was inculcated to everyone that all people live by a single lifestyle and everyone was trying to pretend that everyone was living exactly the same lifestyle as others. So people were pretending that either they do not see individual differences or, if these differences were more than the limits that could be ignored or tolerated, the "guilty" individual was badly isolated from the "mass of unconscious hypocrites." This was an inextricable problem, which today in the pluralist mega space can only be solved with accepting different lifestyles, that is, by deleting the inextricability of the contradiction of different lifestyles. In fact, the solution for these contradictions is obtained by accepting these very contradictions and regarding them as natural or even desirable. But the necessary attitude for adoption of such an approach is passing from monistic outlook to a pluralistic one.

In the eighteenth and nineteenth centuries, within the prevailing universalism, such a pluralist approach did not have a positive background for acceptance. In the classical liberalism, which in here includes Rousseau as well, how was this matter resolved? And what mechanism did it have that was not seen as limiting the liberty at all? Surprisingly enough, not only it wasn't interpreted as a limitation to liberty, but on the contrary, it was interpreted as a revelation for liberty. For them, choosing different lifestyles and moral criterion was a sign of decadence, ignorance, and moral backwardness. Therefore, if the minority were not choosing the reasonable way of the majority, they would brand them as ignorant, superstitious, and backward, which has to be educated.

Six

PLURALISTIC TURNAROUND

The early pioneers of liberalism almost saw all the positive values incarnated in liberty. Some of them today are seen as irrelevant. This may be due to the fact that a team of words that are close to the strong values always are used by different social groups for justifying their interests. In the Middle Ages, different social groups used the word "God" in different textures to justify their demands and their interests. In the Age of Reason, they did this by the word "reason" and by showing the reasonableness of their interests. In the age of liberty, liberty was confiscated for good by different classes and social groups and for justifying their interests. It was used in showing the acceptability of the ways they chose for providing those interests.

Isaiah Berlin and Pluralism

When Isaiah Berlin began to deal with the kinds of liberty, his idea reflected the problem briefly pointed to in the above. Classical connotations of liberty were in crisis while new interpretations of liberty were approaching toward pluralism. Not only national and anti-colonial liberation movements, as well as international communist movement, had proliferated totally contradictory connotations vis-à-vis liberal connotations of liberty, but liberalism and its connotations from liberty were also in crisis from within. The later developments showed that a common interpretation of liberty neither exists nor can it exist. Liberty now was neither unified nor universal, but it had become a private matter, that is, freedom in choosing different lifestyles. An important part of the political philosophy of Berlin forms from his scrutiny in separating two kinds of liberty. He says the kind of liberty that emphasizes individual rights is a new and modern one while it was the subject of communal rights in the past:

> Condorcet had already remarked that the notion of individual rights was absent from the legal conceptions of the Romans and Greeks; this seems to hold equally of the Jewish, Chinese and all other ancient civilizations that have since come to light. The domination of this ideal has been the exception rather than the rule, even in the recent history of the west. Nor has liberty in this sense often formed a rallying cry for the great masses of mankind. The desire not to be impinged upon, to be left to oneself, has been a mark of high civilization on the part of both individuals and communities. The sense of privacy itself, of the area of personal relationships as something sacred in its own right, drives from a conception of freedom which, for all its religious roots, is scarcely older, in its developed state, than the Renaissance or the Reformation. Yet its decline would mark the death of a civilization, of an entire moral outlook.[123]

Berlin, in dangers and precipices that classical definitions of liberty carry, carefully wants to reach to a definition of liberty as a safe place, a definition of liberty that is possibly free from error and cannot become against itself:

> The most eloquent of all defenders of freedom and privacy, Benjamin Constant, who had not forgotten the Jacobin dictatorship, declared that at the very least the liberty of religion, opinion, expression, properly must be

---

[123]   Isaiah Berlin, "Two Concepts of . . .", in *Four Essays on Liberty*, 201.

guaranteed against arbitrary invasion. Jefferson, Burke, Paine, Mill compiled different catalogues of individual liberties.[124]

The idea of differentiation of liberty into positive and negative, even if Berlin would not be its founder, entered in political literature only after his famous article *Two Concepts of Liberty* (1968):

> The freedom which consists in being one's own master, and the freedom which consists in not being prevented from choosing as I do by other men, may, on the face of it, seem concepts at no great logical distance from each other—no more than negative and positive ways of saying much the same thing. Yet the "positive" and "negative" notions of freedom historically developed in divergent directions, not always by logically reputable steps, until, in the end, they came into direct conflict with each other.[125]

In *What's Wrong with Negative Liberty* (1979), Charles Taylor says,

> Doctrines of positive freedom are concerned with a view of freedom which involves essentially the exercising of control over one's life. On this view, one is free only to the extent that one has effectively determined oneself and the shape of one's life. The concept of freedom here is an exercise-concept. By contract, negative theories can rely simply on an opportunity-concept, where being free is a matter of what we can do, of what it is open to us to do, whether or not we do anything to exercise these options.[126]

---

[124] Ibid., 198.
[125] Ibid., 203.
[126] Charles Taylor, "What's Wrong with Negative Liberty?" (1979), in *Philosophical Papers* (volume 2) (Cambridge University Press, 1999), 213.

Berlin's differentiation of positive and negative liberty was an important turnaround in the history of ideas about liberty. He published his ideas at a time when the memory of fascist atrocities was still fresh, and the atmosphere of European intelligentsia was deeply under the influence of Marxism, which was strongly respected. A few intellectuals dared to oppose it. The USSR had emerged from the burning furnace of the great patriotic war against fascism as the largest country and one of the world's two military superpowers. And despite the revelations of atrocities of the Stalin's era by Khrushchev, Leninism still had deep roots among the European intellectuals. Therefore, under those conditions, it was not so easy to question the credibility of Marxism. "But the intellectual opinion[127] was largely dominated by Marxist doctrines which represented the liberal epoch as only a phase in a global development towards socialism. By the 1930s, indeed, there were few leaders of opinion who did not consider themselves critics or opponents of liberalism."[128]

At that time, liberty as a political slogan had a vast spectrum with heterogeneous and contradictory extremes that included both individual liberties and the liberation of proletariat and oppressed nations the way it was emphasized in the Marxist tradition. The liberal impression of liberty at that time, in comparison with Marxist impression from liberty (liberty from the domination of private property and the old relations of production), did not have that many advocates.

Berlin did not have much hope about the future of liberty at the time of the writing of this treatise:

> It may be that the ideal of freedom to choose ends without claiming eternal validity for them, and the Pluralism of values connected with this, is only the late fruit of our declining capitalist civilization: an ideal which remote

---

[127] Gray here means the English intellectuals. Apparently, it was the same for the continent.

[128] John Gray, *Liberalism (Concepts in Social Thought)*, 36.

ages and primitive societies have not recognized, and one which posterity will regard with curiosity, even sympathy, but little comprehension.[129]

That is why Berlin fluctuates between disappointment and hope. Berlin thus, by putting aside the positive liberty, also abandons the liberal moral philosophy and theories related to values and good and evil and, according to Charles Taylor, devolves this area to the opposition.[130]

Under those circumstances, Berlin was on to make an ingenious work in this treatise so they could not easily ignore it. He believed a liberty-based politics that does not have a strong philosophical backing not only will not have coherence but it may possibly change to its opposite: "Our Philosophers seem oddly unaware of these devastating effects of their activities . . . conducted by a blind scholastic pedantry,[131] politics has remained indissolubly intertwined with every other form of philosophical enquiry."[132]

The differentiation of negative and positive liberty by Berlin happened under a circumstance that the Cold War had started. This differentiation was extremely critical for the liberalism that was exhausted at that time. Isaiah Berlin's lectures were broadcast on television programs of the BBC One. Then the *Guardian* newspaper printed these lectures over six weeks. The Berlin we see in these lectures is a clever politician whose main goal is to convince the audience. He shows that positive liberty is rooted within the classical liberalism itself, but at that time, it was not known that it could lead to such catastrophes. The strongest aspect of his logic is to show that the roots of totalitarian ideas are in the eclectic theories of classical school of liberalism, especially in Rousseau, Comte, and Fichte:

---

[129]   Isaiah Berlin, *Two Concepts of Liberty*, 242.
[130]   Charles Taylor, *What's Wrong with Negative Liberty?*, 213.
[131]   Citing these contemptuous words in those years (1958) was something of a norm. Today, with the development of the horizontal/mutual respect, they resemble as unusual.
[132]   Isaiah Berlin, *Two Concepts of Liberty*, 201.

"Constant saw in Rousseau the most dangerous enemy of individual liberty, because he had declared that 'in giving myself to all, I give myself to none.'"[133]

Berlin does not deny that positive liberty has many amazing attractions. No wonder that many of the thinkers of the classical liberalism could not ignore it. The attraction of the positive liberty is in its invitation to individual effort for liberation from internal constraints and reaching perfection whose outcome is an individual in control of herself.

In chapter four, we noted that philosophers of the Enlightenment fancied that bodily desires would drive out the values that thrived and prevailed in the Christianity of the Middle Ages. In chapter five, we saw that, with the dawn of liberty, many of the old values appeared in a new context and the tolerant man who sought peaceful life and evaded blood and war changed into an idealist, libertarian revolutionary drenched in blood and violence. From then on, the character of Robespierre who linked the chain of revolutionaries from the French Revolution to the October Revolution multiplied, and again, two kinds of reason played much tragic role. During this time, instead of the man who wanted comfort and was a compromising man who was under the attention of English philosophers, a new kind of man was born. The Rousseauian-Marxist revolutionaries committed grave atrocities.

"This was a quality he [Charles Taylor] found in the two teachers who would have the most enduring influence on him, Isaiah Berlin and Iris Murdoch."[134] Maybe this importance that Berlin's thoughts had for Charles Taylor has been his instigation for contemplation in

---

133   Ibid., 235.
134   Nicholas H. Smith, *Charles Taylor—Meaning, Morals, and Modernity* (Polity Press & Blackwell, 2002), 12.

his theories. In order to have a better view of Berlin's theory, I bring another quotation from Charles Taylor criticizing Berlin:

> Thus the application even of our negative notion of freedom requires a background conception of what is significant, according to which some restrictions are seen to be without relevance for freedom altogether, and others are judged as being of greater and lesser importance. So some discrimination among motivations seems essential to our concept of freedom.[135] I want to argue that we cannot defend a view of freedom which does not involve at least some qualitative discrimination as to motive, i.e., which does not put some restrictions on motivation among the necessary conditions of freedom.[136]

It seems that Berlin does not have a convincible answer against this question of Charles Taylor that, if all values become at the same level, how can one defend liberty as the more superior value or common value among men? John Gray also believes that "nothing in Berlin's thought privileges liberalism . . . nothing in Berlin's pluralism shows why freedom of choice should not be only one value among others."[137]

Berlin's thought moves in opposite of Taylor's. In this belief, the problems began when two kinds of selves were separated. Charles Taylor shows that, contrary to Berlin's idea that differentiation of self into base and noble may be an obstacle to the path to liberty, without such a separation, liberty will be without attraction. In other words, in the absence of differentiation of self into base and noble, we lack that strength of distinction and realization that is necessary for the tribute of liberty and its veneration against the lack of liberty.

---

[135] Charles Taylor, "What's Wrong with Negative Liberty?", 219.
[136] Ibid.
[137] John Gray, *Berlin*, 150.

When Isaiah Berlin stood up against the positive liberty and affirmation of negative liberty, the spectrum of different, even contradictory, meanings of liberty practically had prepared a proper background for pluralism. The path Berlin took was chosen very cautiously. He interpreted the liberty as the liberty to choose pluralistic methods of life and kept distance from the classical interpretation of liberty.

In the next step, preparing the path of pluralism, Isaiah Berlin discards the idea of perfection and, by this, entangles himself with some theoretical problems. He essentially says that human beings, with their desires, sensualities, and faults on one hand and their rationality, philanthropy, and justice seeking on the other, and considering the amount of mixing of these varies from one individual to the other has to be the goal of political philosophy. Therefore, it is better:

> [T]o admit that the fulfillment of some of our ideals may in principle make the fulfillment of others impossible, is to say that the notion of total human fulfillment is a formal contradiction, a metaphysical chimera. For every rationalist metaphysician, from Plato to the last disciples of Hegel or Marx, this abandonment of the notion of a final harmony in which all riddles are solved, all contradictions reconciled, is a piece of crude empiricism, abdication before crude facts, intolerable bankruptcy of reason before things as they are, failure to explain and to justify, to reduce everything to a system, which 'reason' indignantly rejects.[138]

Apparently, it seems that, in Berlin's pluralism, the followers of the idea of the fulfillment of human perfection should be denounced and excluded because some of our ideals contradict with some others. If we consider this conclusion of Berlin's ideas as an unwanted slip

---

[138]   Isaiah Berlin, *Two Concepts of Liberty*, 238.

from his side, we should accept that pluralism does not warrant segregation. Pluralism is the gate of a different paradigm that, by entering through it, everyone can follow her own specific desires and lifestyle. In the pluralistic society, different individuals have different desires, and these desires cannot be reconciled with the universal principles of modernity in the old form.

If we accept the above reasoning, a paradox appears. In that case, we have to accept that the advocates of the fulfillment of human perfection have as much right as Berlin himself. Therefore, the advocates of perfection, in order to approach perfection, have to fulfill a segregation act. Basically, the requirements for perfection in any ground are enforcement of segregation and bias. Some things come to the scene; others are eliminated. The meaning of bias and segregation is this very thing.

While in the above, where we took Berlin's statement as unwanted slip, we concluded that pluralism does not allow segregation and bias. The paradox here is that achieving pluralism requires the inclusion of the individuals who believe in the idea of perfection as well. But the idea of perfection inherently includes bias and segregation. On the other hand, bias and segregation are the negation and contradiction of pluralism. Therefore, one can conclude that the statement we quoted from Berlin in the above, where he refuted the advocates of the idea of human perfection, is not an unwanted slip. Perhaps Berlin, for solving this paradox, has concluded that supporting the idea of perfection leads to segregation and bias and this matter does not go with pluralism. But on the other hand, if we discard the advocates of the idea of perfection, pluralism will not be complete. That is, such pluralism in which the advocates of the idea of perfection are not present will be preferential and segregated. Therefore, the advocates of the idea of perfection cannot be discarded from the pluralist mega space, just as the opponents of the idea of perfection and those who are sympathetic with Isaiah Berlin cannot be discarded from the pluralist mega space. What should we do? Perhaps it is with regard to these problems that John Gray writes about the Berlin's pluralism: "It is the question whether pluralism and liberalism may not be, in general or across a large range of historical circumstances, conflicting and competitive in their implications for practice."[139]

Considering Berlin's writings on pluralism, we find he could not see the difference between public sphere and private spaces with clarity and lucidity that is seen today. Nowadays, both the advocates of the idea of human perfection and their opponents dialogue within their related private spaces. That is, these ideas that represent different values can only be credible in their relevant private spaces and cannot defy as universal truths in the public sphere. With a differentiating attitude that separates as such, the above paradox resolves. That is in the framework of the relevant private spaces, that is, in their community, anything can be done because these private spaces/communities are consisted from the individuals who have overlapping values with each other and often would like to live in conformity with their communal values and lifestyles. These lifestyles can never be universal. Those who want to forcibly universalize their communal lifestyles, they would be terrorists if they did not have enough power, and they would be militarist if they had state power. Therefore, segregation and bias are the innate characteristics of private spaces/communities. Passing from space A/community A to space B/community B, what will change are the kinds of biases and directions of the segregations. But none of these can remain in the public sphere.

By and large with regard to the contradictory side of his pluralism and at the same time with the detailed explanations that Berlin has offered in his article, it can be concluded that he is against granting a universal position to the totalitarian ideas, but he does not have any opposition to them being remained in the limits of their private spaces/communities, provided they do not threaten the other spaces/communities. Richard Rorty, regarding this aspect of Berlin's concepts, says that, in general, he was opposed to universalism:

---

[139] John Gray, *Berlin*, 146.

Berlin revivifies the notion of romanticism by opposing it not to classicism but to universalism. He thereby transforms it into one term of a philosophical, rather than a literally, contrast. He calls universalism the "backbone of the main Western tradition" and says that it was that backbone that romanticism "cracked." Romanticism, Berlin says, was "the deepest and most long-lasting of all changes in the life of the West."[140,141]

While one may agree with Rorty's take on Berlin's opposition to universalism, one would consider that Berlin's ideas are not without contradiction. While he was against universalism, he nevertheless wanted the principles of pluralism to have universal credibility. Berlin's difficulty was that, while he ousted the theories that were opposed to pluralism from the public sphere, he was bringing the theories that were for pluralism to the public sphere without identifying where this exclusive right came from.

As we shall see in the next chapter, Rawls had to formulate the theory of "reasonable overlapping consensus" in order to introduce an acceptable public sphere as the only base for "political liberalism." Although I am not sure, it seems that Isaiah Berlin supposes he has a right to announce that pro-pluralism doctrines could occupy the public sphere and be considered for all people as a common language. When we talk about the present pluralist mega space, many religious and nonreligious communities, with a variety of their principles, exist within it next to each other. That is, in the pluralist mega space, one cannot reach any definition of unanimously accepted universal principles. Moreover, there would be no philosophical foundations to support those principles.

---

[140] Isaiah Berlin, *The Roots of Romanticism* (Princeton University Press, 2001), 20-21 and xiii); cited in Richard Rorty, "Grandeur, Profundity, and Finitude," in *Philosophy as Cultural Politics: Philosophical Papers* (volume 4), 80.

[141] Richard Rorty, "Grandeur, Profundity, and Finitude," in *Philosophy as Cultural Politics: Philosophical Papers* (volume 4), 80.

Berlin supposes any effort for reaching a common ground in moral and value subjects as futile. The schools of classical liberalism that were collections of philosophical doctrines with familial similarities that had somehow shared concepts about society, individual, free will, values and ethics, now, by Berlin's formulation, lose a considerable part of their territory like a university that a part of its classes are out of the control of the president of university. From this position of Berlin to the present position of Rorty, who suggests that philosophy in general be completely separated from politics and politics be concentrated on the practical problems that are in front of the contemporary world in a profitable and pragmatic way and without any regard to philosophical foundations, a position that in the past four decades Berlin had attacked with the "blind scholastic pedantry" label, is not that far. John Gray says: "If I am not mistaken, Berlin's liberalism is by far the most formidable and plausible so far advanced, inasmuch as it acknowledge the limits of rational choice and affirms the reality of radical choice."[142]

Isaiah Berlin is the most famous defender of pluralism among the contemporary political philosophers. Berlin's pluralism can be viewed separately from the theoretical and practical points of views. From the theoretical point of view, Berlin's pluralism is an important step in passing from classical liberalism to a liberalism that has incorporated pluralism, although it is not completely free from the contradictions. His class of pluralism opposes monistic theories and philosophies. In his writings, he emphasizes that, if someone is for individual rights and liberties, she has to bid farewell to monistic theories and philosophies and become the serious supporter of the pluralism of humanistic values. From the practical point of view, the subject is totally different. Practical pluralism is an indisputable reality in the present world, and no theory or philosophy, no matter how much is monist, dualist, or pluralist, is incapable of eliminating its rivals. Today, even the most obsolete or outdated ideas and concepts that could be traced in the dust-covered and forgotten books are unexpectedly ˌ

---

[142]   John Gray, *Berlin*, 146.

flourishing and have many supporters. All types of communities, including supernatural, mystic, healers, and abracadabra, are lined up next to all sorts of artistic, literary, pseudoscientific, and scientific circles. In all, the consequences of these realities is that today all living individuals with their ideals, desires, and preferences have apparently become the only criterion of dos and don'ts and good and evil.

It seems that the pluralism of Berlin fits the weak pluralism, that is, the lower phase of the pluralist mega space, that the acute and growing pressure for leaving the domination of the universal principles of the modernity still does not exist. The communities and circles that are forming are based on the different lifestyles are in their early stage. But it may not be responsive for the advanced phase of pluralism that is the strong pluralism.

Pluralism and Its Misunderstandings

The equality of the rights of all spaces/communities within the pluralist mega space will turn into a pivotal element. Based on the principle of equality, a group like the Taliban can also live according to their lifestyles and principles, provided they accept not to use force against the others. Therefore, once we talk about irrevocable and dominant principles, we have to define which space/community we are talking about. Our world consists of masses of all kinds of spaces/communities that their principles are only irrevocable for their indigenous people. But the validity of these principles is simply limited to the walls of these spaces/communities while they are not valid in others. When the people of these spaces/communities dialogue with each other, many misunderstandings occur in between because we do not yet notice to the limits of validity. That is, our principles cannot be applied to the inhabitants of other spaces/communities. Therefore, while we are not familiar with the nature of the pluralist mega space, there would be some misunderstandings for the people of the liberal and illiberal spaces/communities in listening to each other. These misunderstandings may even end in violent atmosphere, as we have confronted now.

The equality for the Taliban's right to live next to the liberals like Berlin stems from the development of the radical equality of the rights of all individuals and communities. Such a radical equality is a new phenomenon. Equal rights of all individuals announced in the classical liberalism and in the American and French Revolutions were not radical equality. That nonradical equality was the consequence of the domination of an ethnocentric outlook that rendered in delegating it to all human beings and as the universal principles. According to this idea, those accepting it would end up having equal rights, but those who were not were opposite to the universal principles and had to be reeducated. Otherwise, they would be suppressed. This is the same position of the Taliban in that you become their brother once you believe in the principles they believe in. Based on these ethnocentric universal principles, neoconservatives were blowing the trumpet of the war or liberty. From this point of view, Richard Rorty saying "we need to peel apart Enlightenment liberalism from Enlightenment rationalism"[143] does not seem justifiable. Despite the fact that Rorty often criticizes the ethnocentricity of the enlightenment, here, he remains an ethnocentric as well.

We should verify whether there is a public sphere in the pluralist mega space. Is there such a public sphere? If it is, can we find or establish some universal principles to have any validity in this public sphere? And if they have validity, what is it based on? That is, we want to know that, in the pluralist mega space, how one can render universal principles and basically if such a thing is possible or not.

---

[143] Richard Rorty, "Justice as a Larger Loyalty," in *Philosophy as Cultural Politics: Philosophical Papers* (volume 4), 55.

SEVEN

ARCHIMEDIAN RELYING STAND
OF PLURALISM

(Politics in Public Sphere and Philosophy in Private Spaces)

" It is a great puzzle to me why political liberalism was not worked out much earlier . . . Does it have deep faults that preceding writers may have found in it that I have not seen."[144] Up to the recent decades, pluralism was regarded as a temporary or unnatural condition that eventually has to change toward monism. By relying on this belief that "truth is unique but not-truths are many," a single and solid truth would drive away different ideas. But it seems that gradually during recent decades, the advocates of pluralism have been increased daily. Now monistic reason, after almost two thousand years of dominance, finally has tuned with pluralism, and we are witnessing the new paradigm of pluralistic reason and pluralistic rationality. Now in the domain of political philosophy, the active schools have to tune themselves with pluralism. Today in general, none of the political philosophers (and among them the philosophers who refute the need for political philosophy), have not the possibility of being considered as serious without approaching pluralism.

But entering pluralist mega space also necessitates redefining political philosophy itself. In response to Habermas, Rawls contemplates the hidden difference of political philosophy in *Political Liberalism* with the old model of political philosophies:

---

[144]   P.L. Rawls, footnote, 374.

> The more familiar view of political philosophy is that
> its concepts, principles and ideals, and other elements
> are presented as consequences of comprehensive
> doctrines—religious, metaphysical, and moral. By contrast,
> political philosophy, as understood in political liberalism,
> consists largely of different political conceptions of right
> and justice viewed as *freestanding*.[145]

Reading Richard Rorty's article, *The Priority of Democracy to Philosophy* (1988), one may think that there is not much difference between Rorty and Rawls about the relation between philosophy and democracy. From Rorty's point of view, political concepts of citizens stem from their utilitarian and pragmatic foundations. Rorty's position, despite his emphasis on liberty and creativity of the individuals on one hand and the necessity of human solidarity on the other, is somehow far from the respect for the others. According to Rorty, religious, moral, and philosophical concepts have to be thrown out of the political domain because nothing good comes from their interior. They, in their most optimistic condition, are private games of the citizens that should not be brought into the public sphere. It seems that, on some occasions, Rorty is not attentive to the inner motives and incentives of the people who are active in a society. These inner motives and incentives normally are interwoven with the moral, religious, and philosophical symbols. We cannot separate and isolate the utilitarian and pragmatic side of these conglomerated bodies.

For Rawls, diversity and incoherence of comprehensive doctrines among citizens is a respectable and accepted principle. Rawls accepts this. Not only does he see any problem in it, he even evaluates it as positive. When his opponents accuse Rawls that he is placed in the danger of moral relativism and lack of noble human values, he says that citizens, by relying on their comprehensive doctrines, have reached a common political program in a reasonable overlapping consensus. The type of argument that a religious person employs in

---

[145]   John Rawls, *Political Liberalism*, 374.

order to justify the necessity of a democratic society and the reasons he brings for justifying and interpreting this necessity may not be too similar with that of another religious or nonreligious person. Rawls sees all these points. That is why he opens place for all of them in his theories.

According to Rawls, in a democratic society, religion, morality, philosophy, art, and so forth are strong and active among citizens, and they should be handled with most care and respect. Basically, the nature of contemporary democratic societies is such that one cannot necessarily reduce this pluralism in religious, moral, and philosophical doctrines with education or negotiation to a single one. The only way out of such a dilemma is acceptance of pluralism in the grounds of stands and, at the same time, search in the grounds of unity, not in the level of philosophies and doctrines but in the level of politics. Rawls's theory is not a rival to religious, moral, and philosophical doctrines of citizens, but it is a tool for reaching to what Rawls names the "reasonable overlapping consensus."

Rawls believes that citizens with different and incongruous doctrines can reach consensus around a single political program. Citizens contemplate their own reasons for their doctrines, and these reasons are so different and even incoherent that concentrating on them has no use and does not lead to a single doctrine. The point that is important is that they can reach a "reasonable overlapping consensus" with different and even contradictory reasons. With a little negligence, one can assume that, in the theoretical system of Rawls, this "reasonable overlapping consensus" is the Archimedean relying stand of the contemporary pluralist mega space.

Contrary to the Age of Enlightenment, the private domain has now acquired a great importance. That religion, morality, and philosophy have become private is not to mean that they have lost their importance. Rather, they are very important such that, if they want to take them to the public sphere and suggest for all the citizens the same attitude toward them, it would end up in chaos. The present reasonable consensus that exists in the political domain, at least in the West, would end in crisis. In *Political Liberalism*, Rawls repeatedly emphasizes "a political conception of justice is what I call freestanding when it is not presented as derived from, or as part of any comprehensive doctrine. Such a conception of justice in order to be a moral conception must contain its own intrinsic normative and moral ideal"[146]

In the "well-ordered society" of Rawls, illiberal attitudes do not play an important role. Today, it is difficult to come to defend universal principles and realize the world is limited to the democratic West. Therefore, we should offer a different definition from the past, and this definition has to have the capacity to accept and include different, even opposite, lifestyles that manifest in the communities, which may be seen as not reasonable from the point of view of Rawls.

In the classical liberalism, the presence of what we term as the "public sphere" with united and common beliefs among all people and the capability of being attributed all over the world was obvious. Locke aimed only to change the beliefs of public sphere and to regulate it according to the principles of liberalism. In here, the precedence is with Isaiah Berlin, who reached pluralism before Rawls and distanced himself from the classical liberalism. But Berlin remains in that very gate of pluralism and could not offer a different public sphere in the way Rawls have found it. Berlin could not find a reliable stand for his pluralism. Perhaps this deficiency in his works that is seen clearer today was intentional and stems from the lack of his belief in universals.

From Rawls's point of view, the public sphere with the meaning it had in the classical liberalism, that is, a sphere based on a comprehensive doctrine, does not exist, and if it existed in the past, that was nothing other than a private space or a family of private spaces that, by suppressing and undermining the rivals and by relying and emphasizing a totalitarian concept, could drape around its private nature and be accepted as the public sphere:

> In the society of the Middle Ages, more or less united
> in affirming the Catholic faith, the Inquisition was not

---

[146]   Ibid., xliv

an accident; its suppression of heresy was needed to preserve the shared religious belief. The same holds, we suppose, for any comprehensive philosophical and moral doctrine, even secular ones. A society united on a form of utilitarianism, or on the moral views of Kant or Mill, would likewise require the oppressive sanctions of state power to remain so.[147]

Rawls points to the social fermentation that paved the way for a democratic consensus: As Catholic and Protestant, clashed in the Reformation; and these already included a doctrine of the good-the good of salvation. But . . . there was no resolution between them, as their competing transcendent elements do not admit of compromise . . . Circumstance and exhaustion lead to a *modus vi.vendi*: equal liberty of conscience and freedom of thought . . . may sometimes lead to a constitutional, and then to an overlapping consensus.[148]

From Rawls-ian point of view, in a well-ordered society that many reasonable comprehensive religious philosophical and moral doctrines are active among the citizens, instead of a public sphere based on a single comprehensive doctrine, one public sphere based on a freestanding political conception of justice constitutes in the presence of an spectrum of reasonable comprehensive doctrines of citizens, and the citizens who have comprehensive but reasonable doctrines reach a consensus around a political concept. He calls this consensus the "reasonable overlapping consensus." Maybe it is justifiable if one says that, according to Rawls's belief, this reasonable overlapping consensus is the relying stand of the public sphere.

---

[147] Rawls, *Justice as Fairness*, 34.
[148] Rawls, *Political Liberalism*, xl-xli.

Rawls accentuates that this "reasonable overlapping consensus" is not the outcome of the common points of the reasonable comprehensive doctrines:

> To find this political conception we do not look at known comprehensive doctrines with the aim of striking a balance or average between them, nor do we attempt to strike a compromise with a sufficient number of those doctrines actually existing in society by tailoring the political conception to fit them.[149] Citizens do not look into the content of others' doctrines, and so remain within the bounds of the political. Rather, they take into account and give some weight to only the fact-the existence-of the reasonable overlapping consensus itself.[150]

Again about the foundation of public sphere, he says, "The fact that those who affirm the political conception start from within their own comprehensive view, and hence organize their doctrine using different premises and grounds, does not make their affirming it any less religious, philosophical, or moral, as the case may be."[151]

Let us see how Rawls approaches the horizontal/mutual respect:

> We suppose, then, that one task of political philosophy—its practical role, let's say—is to focus on deeply disputed questions and to see whether, despite appearances, some underlying basis of philosophical and moral agreement can be uncovered. Or if such a basis of agreement can not be found, perhaps the divergence of philosophical and moral opinion at the root of decisive political difference can at least be narrowed to that social cooperation on

---

[149] Ibid., xlvii.
[150] Ibid., 387.
[151] Rawls, *Justice as Fairness*, 195.

a footing of mutual respect among citizens can still be maintained.[152]

Rawls clearly has stated this point:

> The diversity of reasonable comprehensive religious, philosophical, and moral doctrines found in modern democratic societies is not a mere historical condition that may soon pass away; it is a permanent feature of the public culture of democracy.[153]

Also, we may attention to this:

> Note that, given the fact of reasonable pluralism, a well-ordered society in which all its members accept the same comprehensive doctrine is impossible. But democratic citizens holding different comprehensive doctrines may agree on political conceptions of justice. Political liberalism holds that this provides a sufficient as well as the most reasonable basis of social unity available to us as citizens of a democratic society.[154]

Maybe it would not be unreasonable if we assume that, according to Rawls, the "reasonable overlapping consensus" is the same thing that creates public sphere and expands it. Of course, such an overlapping consensus does not stem from suppression of other doctrines by a superior doctrine because this consensus is acquired through democratic method:

> We do not deny that vanity and greed, the will to dominate and the desire for glory are prominent in politics and

---

152 Ibid., 2.
153 Rawls, *Political Liberalism*, 36.
154 Rawls, *Justice as Fairness*, 33.

affect the rise and fall of nations. Yet since we can not as a democracy use state power, with its attendant cruelties and corruptions of civic and cultural life, to eradicate diversity, we look for a political conception of justice that can gain the support of a reasonable overlapping consensus to serve as a public basis of justification.[155]

So, I may dare to say that the relying stand of the Rawls-ian public sphere is not a unique standpoint. Rather, it is constituted from a plurality of overlapping stands, that is, a "reasonable overlapping consensus." But these overlapping stands are practically the outcome of a plurality of reasonable comprehensive doctrines that are prevalent among the citizens, and these religious, moral, and philosophical doctrines reach with their own way of reasoning to a common political stand. If citizens are supposed to dialogue with each other so much that they would reach a common stand about the ways and reasons about the necessity of a political program and consequently reach a "reasonable overlapping consensus," they would never reach to any agreement because comprehensive doctrines, when principles are involved, are irreconcilable. But irreconcilability in principles is not an obstacle for these comprehensive doctrines to reach a common stand on a political program. Rawls emphasizes that citizens believe in different comprehensive doctrines. These doctrines inevitably end in the irreconcilable principles. So how can they reach unity on a political program? Will there be something that is not hidden in this process? Let us give two different examples:

+ When the majority of people vote in favor of abortion and turn it into a law, a Christian citizen respects the law, but she does not include this law in her own life. This law is about the public sphere, but she pulls herself apart from this part of the public sphere. She accepts this principle that the majority has the right to turn an important point of their lifestyle into a law. Although

---

[155]   Ibid., 36-37.

she in her privacy looks to those who commit abortion as sinners, she tolerates, even respects, their lifestyle. She does respect the abortion law because it only opens the way to the sinners but does not block the way of the Christians. This law, while it respects the demands of the people who support abortion, does not lead to disrespect their opponents.

In the following example, the law operates differently:

+ The law of banning Islamic veil in public schools of some countries leads to a totally different result. Unlike the abortion law that stops at the limit of the freedom of a Christian, the latter leads to an assault on the limits of individual rights. The law of banning Islamic veil places a Muslim, who does not have the financial means of schooling in private schools, in a crossroad of quitting school or feeling guilt. Not only does it assault the limits of individual liberty, it also violates the principle of respect regarding minorities.

In *Political Liberalism*, Rawls repeatedly uses the word "reasonable" not for limiting the extent of his theory but to put aside the "unreasonable" people and doctrines while he accepts the necessity of their dialogue at the same time. Let us pay attention to this statement (my emphasis):

> Thus, a conception of justice may fail because it can not gain the support of **reasonable** citizens who affirm **reasonable** comprehensive doctrines; or as I shall often say, it can not gain the support of a **reasonable** overlapping consensus. Being able to do this is necessary for an adequate political conception of justice.[156]

---

[156] Rawls, *Political Liberalism*, 36.

About the meaning of the word "reasonable":

> Persons are reasonable in one basic aspect when, among equals say, they are ready to propose principles and standards as fair terms of cooperation and to abide by them willingly, given the assurance that others will likewise do so. Those norms they view as reasonable for everyone to accept and therefore as justifiable to them; and they are ready to discuss the fair terms that others propose. The reasonable is an element of the idea of society as a system of fair cooperation and that its fair terms be reasonable for all to accept is part of its idea of reciprocity.[157]

But the content of the word "reasonable" in different cultures and different societies, especially among the cultures that do not have a Wittgenstein-ian familial resemblances, is not the same at all, such that something that is regarded as reasonable in one culture may be regarded as unreasonable in the other and vice versa. Hence in Rawls's theory, the public sphere that is constituted from the "reasonable overlapping consensus" is constituted actually on a family group of the Western cultures.

In multicultural societies, the public sphere normally is constituted on the hegemony of one culture, for example, the current situation of the United States of America. Therefore in the present condition, it is difficult to speak of a universal public sphere by relying on Rawls's theory. Needless to say, a universalism based on the political or military power no longer is universal.

Rawls uses the word "reasonable" so much, and for putting condition and limiting every case, one can take his word (reasonable) as the meaning of "ours" against "others." In fact, from this point of view, Rawls's position does not have much difference with some of the segregationist doctrines that divide the society into we/our and they/theirs. For Rawls, the word "reasonable," when it is attached as a

---

[157]   Ibid., 49-50.

label to something, means it is acceptable. Or when it is determined that something is "ours," it will be labeled as "reasonable," as if it would be familiarized by labeling this word to anything.

Richard Rorty also agrees with limiting this we/our and they/not ours: "I agree with Rawls about what it takes to count as reasonable, and about what kind of societies we Westerners should accept as members of a global moral community."[158] Rorty's position toward Rawls is a dual position. On one hand, he is for putting aside the cultures that are measured with the Western values' criterion as "they," and on the other, he questions Rawls's neo Kant-ian backgrounds and tries to show that Rawls for offering his theories, whether about "reasonable overlapping consensus" or universalizing his "well-ordered society," does not have any need for these principles. For this, he criticizes Kant-ian moral imperatives: "Obligation, as opposed to trust, enters the picture only when your loyalty to a smaller group conflicts with your loyalty to a larger group."[159] Rorty, in following his critic on Kant, writes:

> What Kant would describe as the resulting conflict between moral obligation and sentiment, or between reason and sentiment, is, on a non-Kantian account of the matter, a conflict between one set of loyalties and another set of loyalties.[160] Moral dilemmas are not, in this view, the result of a conflict between reason and sentiment but between alternative selves, alternative self-descriptions alternative ways of giving a meaning to one's life.[161]

Rawls did not write his *Political Liberalism* only for Westerners. He evidently believed that his theory is applicable to the whole world. "In a paper called 'The Law of Peoples,' Rawls discusses the question

---

158   Richard Rorty, *Justice as a Larger Loyalty*, 55.
159   Ibid., 45. (Rorty quotes the above sentence from a moral philosopher named Baier.)
160   Ibid., 45.
161   Ibid.

of whether the conception of justice he has developed in his books is something peculiarly Western and liberal or rather something universal. He would like to be able to claim universality."[162]

Rawls's books have been translated into the most of world's living languages. Globalization is everywhere. Household appliances have also been globalized. Refrigerators, freezers, washing machines, televisions, and computers have been globalized. It does not come to anyone's mind to localize these household appliances by changing their functions because human needs are universal. If we take Charles Taylor's "first-order" desires/weak evaluation and "second-order" desires/strong evaluation, which was referred to in the previous chapter as the basis of the analysis, more or less, the system of "first-order" desires (food, clothing, sexual, and security needs) are still important throughout the world, while the system of "second-order" desires (desires or evaluations about the system of "first-order" desires) are different from one culture to another. Therefore, if one system of "weak evaluation" is essentially applicable all over the world, collections of "strong evaluation" are all over the world. We may find some resemblance between the system of "weak evaluation" and hardware and between the collections of the "strong evaluation" to the collections of the software. One can install different types of software on a single hardware. The major part of Rawls's theories, using Charles Taylor's terms, are about "strong values," and now that Rawls's theories are spread all over the world, they necessarily should be adjusted to fit with the other cultures. These theories are the product of Western cultures, and now that they have been exported to the whole world, it is quite justifiable to say that these theories have to be properly adjusted to fit the non-Western cultures, just as they were adjusted originally in their birthplace to fit the family of the cultures of the West. These theories are located in the system of "strong values," and they classify and categorize the system of "weak values" in a way that divide them into good/bad and sublime/vile, and not only is this classification and categorization very different from one

---

[162] Ibid., 47.

culture to another, in different cultures, private spaces do not have the same reaction toward them. It may be not quite nonsense if one does speculate that the theories that are related to human sciences, unlike the household appliances, have to be coordinated with the different collections of the strong evaluations.

Rorty writes about this part of Rawls's theories:

> However it emerges that this law [the law of peoples] applies only to *reasonable* peoples, in a quite specific sense of the term "reasonable." The conditions that non-liberal societies must honor in order to be "accepted by liberal societies as members in good standing of a society of peoples" include the following: "its system of law must be guided by a common good conception of justice . . . that takes impartially into account what it sees not unreasonably as the fundamental interests of all members of society."[163]

> Rawls takes the fulfillment of that condition to rule out violation of basic human rights. These rights include "at least certain minimum rights to means of subsistence and security (the right to life), to liberty (freedom from slavery, serfdom, and forced accusations) and (personal) property, as well as to formal equality as expressed by the rules of natural justice" . . . When Rawls spells out what he means by saying that the admissible non-liberal societies must not have unreasonable philosophical or religious doctrines, he glosses "unreasonable" by saying that these societies must "admit a measure of liberty of conscience and freedom of thought, even if these freedoms are not in general equal for all members of society." Rawls' notion of what is reasonable, in short, confines membership

---

[163] Ibid., 48; Quotation from Rawls, *The Law of Peoples*, 81, 61. Cited by Richard Rorty.

of the society of peoples to societies whose institutions encompass most of the hard-won achievements of the West in the two centuries since the Enlightenment.[164]

One can realize that Rorty also sees the global expansion of Rawls's theory to be confronted with serious problems, while he totally agrees with Rawls that the followers of some illiberal cultures and religions, which may be branded as not reasonable, must be put aside from the world community or from the global "reasonable overlapping consensus."

If we are supposed to classify and categorize Western political philosophers from the point of view of familiarity and sympathy they express toward illiberal cultures, Rorty and Rawls certainly, if they don't have a sympathetic view toward them, they absolutely do not share the hard-line position of the neoconservatives. These two philosophers always tried to find ways for reaching and suggesting an understanding of non-Western cultures. But we see that how tide and narrow is the limit to which these philosophers can come to front so the followers of the illiberal cultures like groups like the Taliban can be tolerated. Here we should pay attention to the fact that only one can expect from the followers of illiberal lifestyles to respect others when their lifestyles and views to life and the world be respected in first place. If it is true that the political philosophy of the West still lacks the theoretical base for respecting illiberal outlooks, from here, one can find out how far the neoconservatives, who are not very far from the world's political leadership in the United States, France, and even in Great Britain, are from the threshold of tolerating illiberal cultures.

With small margin of error, one can render a verdict that illiberal cultures will not be able to create the adequate change in the Western theoretical position. We are now inevitably within a transitional period that we may call a catastrophic one, with terrorists and militarists on opposing sides. The reason that militarists and neoconservatives

---

[164] Ibid., 48.

could act with such speed and power during the recent decades to some extent goes back to the ineffectiveness of the present Western political philosophy. But I believe that, sooner or later, some changes will take place in the Western political philosophy toward sympathy with illiberal lifestyles, provided these illiberal communities are based on the association of free individuals who are gathered with their own will and can leave the community when they are not pleased to live according that lifestyle.

This is not necessarily to mean that Western political philosophy would retreat from its present position. But if the methods of fanatic terrorists who live with illiberal lifestyles, in putting pressure for creating theoretical changes in Western political philosophy, have been totally unsuccessful (and, of course, they too did not have this intention), the practical and theoretical resistance of newly emerging illiberal communities that are boiling now throughout the West would be an important factor in expecting my outlook.

Let me finish my book with a phrase from Rawls: "Debates about general philosophical questions can not be the daily stuff of politics ... since what we think their answers are will shape the underlying attitude of the public culture and the conduct of politics."[165]

---

[165] Rawls, *Political Liberalism*, lxi.

I appreciate your comments at bahmanbazargani@yahoo.com.
Attention please: I do not open the attachments.

ABOUT THE AUTHOR

During the Islamic Revolution of Iran, Bahman Bazargani witnessed that a whole nation was initiated in a new faith. It seemed to him as if he was descended among the people who behaved as if they were attracted by a quasi aesthetic focus of attraction. Soon he concentrated in the common trends and biases that demarcated one cultural paradigm from the others. These common trends are out of the will and conscious aims of the people living in that paradigm. He reached to the conclusion that in each cultural paradigm there is a quasi aesthetic focus of attraction that attracts the people living in that paradigm. He started his life-long project a research in the relation between the quasi aesthetic focus of attraction and evolution of man.

In 1995, his philosophical articles, as well as his literary critics, appeared in the literary newspapers, magazines, and periodicals of Tehran, which continued up to the present. His principal book, *Matris-e Zibaee* (*The Matrix of Beauty*), was released in Tehran in 2002. *Fazay-e Novin* (*The New Space*), and *Naghde pluralisti* (*The Pluralist Critic*), were published in Tehran in 2010 and 2012, respectively. *Dialog-hay-e Matrisi* (*THE Matrix-ian Dialogues—Interviews*) and his Political Memories are in the publishing process.

The author has personally revised the text of the English translation of *The New Space*. He has written a new introduction to the English text.

Bahman Bazargani lives in Tehran.